ICONIC RESTAURANTS

of

BUTLER COUNTY

OHIO

TERI HORSLEY

AMERICAN PALATE

Published by American Palate
A Division of The History Press
Charleston, SC
http://www.historypress.net

Front cover (clockwise from top left): Tim Wolf cooking meals at Andy's Restaurant. *Courtesy of Mary Jo Lambros Smallwood*; Original site of Chester's Pizza. *Courtesy of Nick Dadabo*; Richard's Pizza's "Pizza Boy" sending off a shipment of steak sandwiches. *Courtesy of Karen Underwood Kramer*; Original site of Shady Nook. *Courtesy of Teri Horsley*; The Cone. *Courtesy of Keith Wren.*

Back cover: Nick Dadabo preparing a locally famous Chester's pizza. *Courtesy of Nick Dadabo*; *inset*: Richard Underwood serving at Richard's Pizza in 1958. *Courtesy of Karen Underwood Kramer.*

First published 2019

Manufactured in the United States

ISBN 9781467138611

Library of Congress Control Number: 2019932638

Notice: The information in this book is true and complete to the best of our knowledge. It is offered without guarantee on the part of the author or The History Press. The author and The History Press disclaim all liability in connection with the use of this book.

This book is dedicated to the family members of each of the iconic restaurants found within its covers. Without your willingness to share your personal histories, my idea would not have become a reality, and I am truly grateful for each of you and your willingness to participate.

CONTENTS

Contents

PREFACE

Growing up in Butler County, Ohio, offers one a traditional Midwestern existence: Friday night football, the annual county fair, small-town politics and many local restaurants that have been owned by the same family for generations. In my own hometown of Hamilton, the county seat and Butler County's largest city, everyone knew the Milillos, the Isgros, the Nichtings and the Jolivettes (who owned Jolly's). We supported these folks by offering our dining dollars in exchange for their great food, and we often offered our talents in exchange for a place on their staff. In my own experience, my first job—at fifteen—found me working for the Jolivettes as a carhop at their Brookwood Avenue location. I'll never forget the incredibly short uniforms, the giant mugs of root beer, my coworkers and my endless search for the perfect re-creation of their already-perfect footlong hot dog. We debated for hours about the correct blend of cheese and chili, but in the end, we typically went back to the way the recipe was originally created. I have great memories of those early days of my life, and I made great friends, many of whom I still enjoy today.

Likewise, I fondly remember my family's enjoyment of Milillo's cheese pizza every Sunday night throughout the 1970s. The gooey cheese and homemade sauce—topped off by my family's laughter as we caught up on our week—made it a bit easier for this shy teenager to face going back to school on Monday. Later, as I moved toward adulthood, another of my favorite Milillo's memories began, occurring each New Year's Eve. That's when my cousins and I would start the night's festivities around 5:00 p.m., picking up a sixteen-inch cheese and taking that delicious pizza to our grandparents' house for one final meal before the end of the old year. While my grandparents are long gone, and my cousins have moved away, I can't help but feel close to all of them each time I bite into that delectable cheese and homemade Milillo's sauce on top of that freshly baked crust.

Fine dining also played a prominent role in my community, and for my family, there were only a few ways to impress your friends or out-of-town guests when it came to fine dining in Hamilton in the 1970s, '80s and '90s. You took them to Isgro's, Nichting's or Waldo's—it was as simple as that. When I think back on the many birthdays, anniversaries, wedding rehearsal dinners and other special events I enjoyed in these establishments, it saddens me greatly to think about the fact that they are no longer here.

By now, it's probably obvious that my own memories of these and other Butler County, Ohio restaurants are what prompted me to write this book. What has been amazing is that, throughout the process, as I talked to the families who owned the restaurants and bounced ideas off of my own friends about which places to include, I came to understand the true meaning of the word "iconic," and a book title was born. While *Merriam-Webster* defines "iconic" as something that is "widely recognized and well-established," my friends and my memories have expanded that definition to include the Butler County, Ohio restaurants that are part of this book. While space does not allow me to include every regional restaurant that could be deemed iconic, it is my hope that everyone who reads the histories of these selected eateries will remember them with fondness and will take pride in the culinary history that defines our region.

ACKNOWLEDGEMENTS

Thanks to the following:

*The families of each restaurant that is included in this book. Without your help, it would not have been possible
*Lisa Rankey, of Lisa Rankey Photography, for her assistance in converting the photos to meet acceptable publication standards
*David Balsinger, of Balsinger Media, for his help in converting the photos to acceptable publication standards
*Photographer Todd Rice for his work in adding to the overall photographic collection presented here
*The many friends and schoolmates who connected me to the families who owned these iconic restaurants
*My mother, Margaret Hoel, for always being there when I'm frustrated and ready to quit
*And most importantly, to my Lord, Jesus Christ, who is solely responsible for any success that I may have

PROLOGUE

On March 24, 1803, Butler County, Ohio, was formed from part of nearby Hamilton County, which today includes the city of Cincinnati. Named for General Richard Butler, an officer in the Continental army during the Revolutionary War, the county's land was first occupied by successive groups of Native Americans. By 1793, white settlers began moving into the area in large numbers after the signing of the Treaty of Greenville, creating a living boundary between the natives and white Europeans. In particular, it's believed that the earliest white French explorers passed through the area near the Miami River in what is now Liberty Township/West Chester, giving way to an even greater influx of Europeans in the nineteenth and twentieth centuries. Between 1803 and 1823, in particular, the townships became officially recognized by the state of Ohio because of this growth, and large portions of the county's land were even first purchased by nonresident owners, including future president William Henry Harrison. However, as time went along, the immigrants who began buying or renting the county's property as an investment actually began settling here. Likewise, it was this immigration explosion of the late nineteenth and early twentieth centuries that brought what could be described as extreme growth to the county's previously established cities and townships, including Hamilton, Middletown, Oxford and Fairfield. This growth also brought about a desperate need for community services such as retail stores, grocery stores and small family-run restaurants.

Looking at each city's development, it is Hamilton, Butler County's largest city (with an estimated population of 62,092 in 2016), that has the longest background; it was a military fort (established in 1791) before the creation of Butler County. By 1794, a town had grown up around the fort, and the city of Hamilton was born. First known as Fairfield, Hamilton grew quickly and reached a population of just over 1,400 by 1840. In the nineteenth century, Hamilton flourished as many new residents arrived from Ellis Island after emigrating from places like Germany, Ireland and Italy. In particular, the fourth ward of the city—with boundaries along what is now East Avenue, State Route 4, High Street and State Route 127—became a culinary center of sorts, as it was home to many Italian immigrants who began working as bakers, grocers and restaurateurs to support their families while offering food service to the surrounding region.

To the north of Hamilton, Butler County's second largest city, Middletown, was incorporated by the Ohio General Assembly in 1833, becoming an official city in 1886. With less than 10,000 people residing in Middletown for much of the nineteenth century, the dawn of the twentieth brought the arrival of Armco (1899), a major steel company, and with it came a population boom that has remained relatively stable for decades. With a 2016 population of 48,813, it was the rapid growth originally attributed to Armco that helped the company become one of Butler County's largest employers and helped Middletown enjoy its heyday in the mid-twentieth century. Likewise, with that rapid growth came a need for local restaurants to serve Armco's employees and their families. As such, a few hot spots that were built and specifically designed to attract those workers remain open today.

The charter of Miami University in 1809 brought Oxford, Ohio, into being, and though the original village incorporation came in February 1830, Oxford did not gain city status until 1971. In spite of its relatively small permanent population of 21,943 (as of 2016), the growth originally brought about by Miami University (and eventually the Western College for Women) created a need for higher-end restaurants both in town and in the surrounding region. This growth came at the same time as the increase in the popularity of the American supper club in the 1930s, '40s and '50s, and as a result, many fine-dining restaurants popped up in Oxford and the surrounding townships. These clubs brought in the locals but also drew people who had traveled to the area from across the country.

Finally, it wasn't until 1955 that the city of Fairfield was incorporated, although what was first known as Fairfield Township back in 1803 provided easy access to the region thanks to a trolley line at the city's Symmes Corner intersection located along what is now State Route 127. It was this access to a trolley that brought folks to Fairfield Township, as it connected Cincinnati to the south and Dayton to the north. Because of the influx of regional travelers, the area had many fine dining and pub options, such as Symmes Tavern and The Milders Inn.

With a history rich in the aforementioned industrialization, higher education and a huge immigration boom (and the creation of many iconic restaurants as a result), today, Butler County, Ohio, is a culinary center that is often overlooked because of its close proximity to the larger cities of Cincinnati and Dayton. However, with many of these restaurants having a personal history that dates back well over one hundred years, the iconic restaurants of Butler County deserve a place in the annals of dining history, as each has brought great food, great family and great memories to the patrons who have supported them for decades. In addition to this longevity, at a time when so many restaurants can't survive the first year, this particular group has played a major role in the development of the local food culture, and as such, it is important that the stories of the restaurants—and the people behind them—be shared and enjoyed.

PART I

PIZZA, FINE DINING AND THE ITALIAN CONNECTION

1

FROM ELLIS ISLAND TO BUTLER COUNTY

IN SEARCH OF THE AMERICAN DREAM

In the 1880s, more than three hundred thousand Italian immigrants emigrated from their homeland to America, and most of them came through Ellis Island. Ten years later, that number doubled, and by the early twentieth century, over four million Italian immigrants lived on American soil. In fact, by the dawn of the 1920s, 10 percent of America's foreign-born population came from Italy, and though there were many—often complex—reasons for this mass immigration, at its core, it seemed to tie into the lack of a unified citizenry at home. Widespread poverty, violence and social chaos had been going on in Italy for decades, and many of the country's poorest citizens (especially those in the rural south and on the island of Sicily) had little hope for improvement. With this mass poverty and a struggling new government, disease began to spread, making the situation even worse. At the same time, transatlantic transportation became possible, and word of American prosperity came from returning immigrants who were fortunate enough to have already ventured west. Because of the hopelessness in their homeland and the beacon of hope that seemed to define the United States at that time, millions of Italians decided to venture out in search of the American dream, with many being single men who intended to return home within three to five years.

However, as skilled farmers and laborers, many ended up staying and seeking out any kind of stable work they could find. Likewise, many also stayed in contact with their relatives back home, sending money to support them. As such, the Library of Congress reports that right around the start of the twentieth century, Italian immigrants sent between $4 and $30 million back to Italy, and as a result, an increase in wealth in the former, poorer sections of the country can be directly tied to money earned by their immigrant relatives living in the United States.

After crossing the Atlantic Ocean, the first thing most of these Italians saw was the Statue of Liberty in New York Harbor. Though the arrival at Ellis Island must have been exhilarating for them, there was also the very real fear of having to convince immigration inspectors that they would not cause trouble and were worthy of being accepted as citizens. After passing through quarantine, the ships were met by immigration officials who were ready to inspect the passengers. These officials were called "groupers" by the Italians, as they ordered them to form two lines as they got off the ship, with women and children in one and men in the other. Each person was tagged with a color-coded slip of paper that indicated the steamship line and included a manifest number and the immigrant's name. The process was often very difficult for the immigrants but was necessary to handle the up to two thousand people who often arrived at the harbor at one time. After this grouping, the next step was the medical inspection, historically known as the "line inspection." Basically, one charge doctor would examine each immigrant from eyes to scalp and neck from the front and profile. Each person was checked for signs of mental instability and disease, and a thorough scrutiny of the person's walk, posture and mannerisms occurred. After this full examination, three doctors were then asked to sign off on the immigrant's medical certificate, and if a person was found to be very sick or unstable, they would be sent to receive medical care and/or treatment before being forced to undergo the whole process again.

After the grouping and medical inspection, the Italian immigrants (and others) were taken to a place called the registry room, and anyone who was deemed to be a convicted criminal or a radical or who had a contagious condition that wasn't picked up on the medical exam was rejected and not allowed to enter the country. Those who were accepted often had testimonials of good character written by officials in Italy as well as telegrams from the foreign police assuring that the person had not been in trouble with the law. Each immigrant was asked a series of twenty-nine questions about their name, age, occupation, country of origin, next of kin, final destination and if they understood, read or spoke English (many did not). About 80 percent of the Italians (as well as those of other nationalities) who made it to this point were granted entry into America. They were then sent to the ground floor of the registry room to wait for a ferry to transport them to Manhattan or the Jersey City Railway Terminal. Most of those who were detained were released and granted entry into the country within a day or two, however, some were forced to wait weeks before receiving a final decision. During that time, men and women stayed in separate quarters, often breaking up families. Organizations such as the Italian Welfare League and the Society for the Protection of Italian Immigrants (made up of those immigrants who had emigrated to the United States) were the only source of help for those forced to wait.

Once the Italian immigrants passed through Ellis Island, many settled in New York City. At first, they were likely to take construction jobs digging tunnels, building bridges and laying railroads. Since many of those who stayed in New York intended to eventually return to Italy, they did not venture into other parts of the United States. However, some Italians did decide to stay in America because of family members who had already settled here or because they believed that life in the United States would always be better than it was back home. Many of the members of this group eventually found their way to Butler County, Ohio, and their individual experiences have kept them here for generations.

FINDING A NEW HOME IN BUTLER COUNTY

Of the four million Italian immigrants who called the United States home by 1920, over sixty thousand of them left New York and came to Ohio. At first, most found jobs as day laborers for construction companies, although many eventually found employment as waiters, waitresses and cooks. The more successful of these Italians established their own businesses, many in the food service industry, opening grocery stores, bakeries and restaurants that provided their fellow immigrants with the foods that made up their diet back home. Specifically, a large migration of Italian families arrived in Cincinnati, a city that, according to the National Italian American Federation, is still ranked in the top fifty cities in the United States in terms of the size of its Italian population. Cincinnati, located just twenty-five miles from Butler County, was attractive to immigrants, as there were plenty of companies that had jobs for them. As thousands flocked to what is known as the Queen City, there developed pockets of Italian communities, with many folks being related or attending a local Catholic church together. However, despite this new sense of Italian community, Cincinnati was first a city for German immigrants, and as time went on, the Italians started to feel unwelcome. As a result, many moved to surrounding areas—like Butler County—due to having relatives or friends here, and the city of Hamilton, as the largest in the county, ended up being one of their most desired locations.

Once in Hamilton, most of the Italian immigrants settled in the fourth ward of town, as other districts were already being inhabited by immigrants from other lands. The area then, as today, was primarily a working-class neighborhood, and it wasn't long before the more notable Italian families began to open businesses to ensure their bright futures. Likewise, as the second-largest city in the county, Middletown also saw the arrival of many Italian families, and they, too, began to open restaurants to serve their fellow countrymen who desperately missed the food from back home.

For families like the Milillos, the Dadabos, the Isgros and the Schiavones, Butler County, Ohio, became their home and ensured the futures of their offspring. As such, their businesses grew, their restaurants thrived and their products became so popular that people from across the country grew to love them. Now that several generations have passed, the descendants of many of these families still call Butler County home. Likewise, several of the families have passed their businesses to these descendants, and some of these restaurants are still in operation. Although times have changed, and as a result, the restaurants have been forced to make small adjustments to succeed, all of the owners agree that their basic adherence to the recipes created by their ancestors is what has kept them in business for all these years. Each of these families also have their own stories about their family's immigration experience and how the tough times led them to open the restaurants that led to their eventual success. Ultimately, as that distant past gave way to the present, it is abundantly clear that each of these Italian children, grandchildren and even some great-grandchildren are fulfilling their forefathers' original quest to pursue the American dream.

2

MILILLO'S PIZZA

FROM BAKERY TO GROCERY STORE TO PIZZA

In 1909, four brothers left Sammichele di Bari (Saint Michael, Bari), Italy, a town/commune (similar to a township) in the province of Bari in the region of Apulia, southern Italy, which is near the island of Sicily. As with most Italian immigrants in the early twentieth century, the four brothers left this troubled region of their homeland to pursue the success that America promised. The oldest, Francesco Milillo, arrived along with Filippo, Giacomo and Dante at Ellis Island speaking no English. After being admitted to the United States, the brothers made their way to West Virginia, where they worked in the coal mines, an existence that was difficult but allowed them to survive. It was there that Francesco hired a woman to teach them English, understanding that the only way to achieve success in this new world was to begin by learning the language. After a few years, the four brothers made their way to the fourth ward of Hamilton, Ohio, the section of town that was heavily populated by Italian immigrants. Francesco, hungry for the food of his homeland, opened a bakery on Second Street. Being the oldest instilled in Francesco a determination for his family to fit in and succeed in Hamilton, so he changed his name to an Americanized version—Frank. He then decided to marry a woman who shared his Italian heritage but who was born an American citizen. Frank Milillo, Francesco's grandson (who insisted that

Italians don't use surnames like junior or the third), picked up the story from there:

> *My grandma was the only one of this generation of my family that was born here in the United States. Concetta Helena Rizzo was born in Cincinnati and worked in the Sixth Street market there. My grandpa understood the importance of marrying an American girl if an Italian immigrant was to succeed in America, and after meeting her in that market, they fell in love and were married. In spite of grandpa's success, grandma hated the bakery business and wanted a grocery store. So, after she agreed to move to Hamilton, grandpa agreed to open a grocery, located first at Seventh and Ludlow Streets. Shortly thereafter, my grandpa was drafted into the Italian army, and his father insisted he go back to Italy to serve. He honored his father's wishes and returned home to fight with the Italians in World War I, leaving my grandma to sell groceries from the second floor window of their store during the devastating 1913 flood.*

Frank (Francesco) Milillo didn't stay in Italy, deciding instead to return to Ellis Island in 1914 so he could begin the immigration process all over again before returning to Hamilton to rejoin his wife in the running of their store. Because of the devastation to their grocery that occurred in that 1913 flood, the Milillos were forced to relocate to Eleventh and Ludlow Streets, where the grocery remains today.

Over time, as his business success grew, Milillo's entrepreneurial spirit grew with it, and he opened Frank Milillo Distributing across the street. His grandson Frank, who runs the grocery store today, said that in the early twentieth century, Frank Milillo Distributing provided food for all of the small grocery stores in Butler County. Sadly, Frank (Francesco) Milillo died of a heart attack at age fifty-two after fathering six children. By this point, his brother Giacomo, who never Americanized his name, had permanently returned to Italy after World War I to care for his aging father. His brother Filippo, who chose the American name Phil, continued to operate the bakery that he had taken over when Frank bought the grocery store. Dante, who became Dan, ended up running a saloon at Fifth and Henry Streets, and Frank's wife, Concetta, who chose the American name Katie, continued to run the grocery while caring for her family. Frank Milillo (grandson) said that like his grandfather, his grandmother also understood the importance of fitting in with the local culture:

Left: Milillo's Grocery Store, 2018. *Courtesy of Frank Milillo.*

Right: Original meat scale at Milillo's Grocery Store. *Courtesy of Teri Horsley.*

> *My grandma took the name Katie because her next door neighbor in Cincinnati, an Irish woman, called her that. Though she was born here in the States, her parents were not, and they instilled in her the idea that it was important for Italians to Americanize as soon as possible after arriving. As a result, Concetta Helena became what she thought was the fine American name of Katie and continued to go by that name for the rest of her life.*

As Katie continued to run the Milillo's grocery store, the death of her husband forced her son Tony Milillo to take over the distributing company at the age of eighteen. (As an aside, later, in World War II, Tony Milillo worked for General George Patton as a supply sergeant in the U.S. army and was on the team that liberated Auschwitz in 1945.) Katie Milillo still owned the various Milillo properties left to her by her husband, and she successfully ran the grocery for much of the rest of her life, not retiring until 1977, when she was in her eighties. Her son, also named Frank (and the father of the aforementioned grandson), and his wife, Audrey, took over at that point, running the grocery until Frank died in 2014. It was then that their son—once again, the aforementioned grandson, Frank—returned to Hamilton, leaving his career in corporate America and partnering with his sister Elaine (a railroad engineer) to keep the store alive:

> *I am Frank Vito Milillo, the son of Frank Vito Milillo, who was the son of Frank Vito Milillo. As a result, because of our history, I, along with my sister, just wanted to keep this grocery going after my grandfather and father passed on. This was my grandmother Katie's American dream, and when all else failed over the course of time, this store fed my family and continues to feed this part of the Hamilton community as it has for over one hundred years. When my grandfather ran this store, he helped everybody in this neighborhood. When other Italian immigrants arrived, he gave many of them their first American job. Later on, when my dad ran this store, he, too, was everybody's best friend, and he even built a baseball field on his property at Thirteenth and Maple so the neighborhood kids had a place to play. When dad died, people around the neighborhood owed him thousands of dollars in credit that he had extended, but he wanted to support the local people, as well as their kids and grandkids, so he never complained or tried to collect.*

THE ARRIVAL OF MILILLO'S PIZZA

As Francesco Milillo and his descendants ran the family grocery store, his brother Filippo (who became known as Phil) turned the family bakery into a huge success. What began in the early part of the twentieth century as a small family operation became a huge production bakery after Phil moved the business to Heaton Street in 1912. As time went on, the bakery provided most of Butler County's restaurants with their bread products, and it even made the bread for all of the county schools.

Before moving to Hamilton and running his bakery, Phil Milillo began his career around 1909 in Cincinnati, shortly after immigrating from Italy, by working for a cousin selling bread and sausages off of a street cart. Recently, Ron Stout—the husband of Stasia Milillo, Phil's granddaughter (Ron and Stasia currently own Milillo's Pizza, which evolved from the bakery)—said that when that bakery closed after being run by Phil's children (including his oldest son, Jack), the making of the Italian pizza of their homeland was the next logical step, and a new business plan was born:

The Milillos knew pizza because of the success of the bakery, and the family branched off, eventually owning two local pizza restaurants, one of which was Milillo's. When a family knows baking, it is easy to transition to pizza, and with their own creation of the sauce that we still use and the dough that we still bake fresh every day, it is easy to understand why Milillo's Pizza has been a success since it opened fifty years ago.

It was Phil Milillo's son Jack (the father of Stasia), born in 1916, who was the force behind the success of Milillo's Pizza. Though he didn't officially open the pizza restaurant until 1968, Jack learned his trade by working in his father's bakery, and as a natural promoter, he understood the importance of holding a notable position in the local community. For example, over the years, Jack purchased the grand champion steer and other livestock at the Butler County Fair every year for use on his menu. Likewise, he never varied from the recipes of his ancestors when it came to his food. Serving only pizza, spaghetti, ravioli, lasagna and salad, Jack kept Milillo's menu the same until he died, and nothing was changed until his son-in-law Ron Stout took over the business in 1996. In an effort to compete with other restaurants that were expanding their product lines, it was Ron who added the cannelloni, manicotti and calzones that Milillo's fans enjoy today. However, he also remained firm in his decision to do nothing to change the Milillo's pizza sauce and product. When asked for his opinion about the success of Milillo's, Stout also attributed it to the trajectory that the various Milillos properties took before they finally ended up at one restaurant that is now located near their original home on Main Street:

In 1968, Milillo's opened at 990 Main Street in Hamilton, the current home of Pfefferle Tire & Auto, but within the first year, Pud, the man who owned the local Gulf station, moved across the street from his corner lot at 1010 Main. Jack thought that was a more prominent location, so he moved up the block to where Milillo's is located today. Starting in 1972, Jack was looking to expand, as his brothers wanted to leave the business, so he first opened a walk-up restaurant in the strip mall that is located on Nilles Road at State Route 127 in Fairfield. Next, he decided to branch into sit-down dining and moved to the other end of that strip center after his other family members were gone. When Milillo's Fairfield closed in 1992, this location on Hamilton's Main Street remained the only one.

Milillo's Pizza, Main Street, Hamilton location (1968–2018). *Courtesy of Todd Rice.*

After Jack Milillo died in 1989, Milillo's Pizza was owned by his wife, Ruth, for just one year before the property was put into the hands of a trustee. Finally, Ron Stout and his wife, Jack Milillo's daughter Stasia, took over a few years later. Returning to the Milillo's Bakery roots from over eighty years before, Ron and Stasia decided to add homemade cookies and pies to the menu, baking everything fresh and on site.

Likewise, Ron and Stasia's daughter Leisel joined the team when she reached adulthood, allowing her mother to retire, and currently, Ron and Leisel make all of the breads, rolls and pizza dough from scratch every day. Ron said it was this decision to continue to offer fresh, homemade products to the local marketplace—combined with the many local, long-term customers—that has kept Milillo's Pizza in business for all these years:

> *I will never use conveyor ovens in here, and I will continue to produce all of our food in the old way. We are built for taste and not speed. The flavors of our product don't mesh with a mass-produced system, and we will continue to operate as a "mom-and-pop" restaurant. It is because of our decision to adhere to this old-world style of doing things that I believe has continued the success that Jack had so many years ago. Likewise, we have loyal customers*

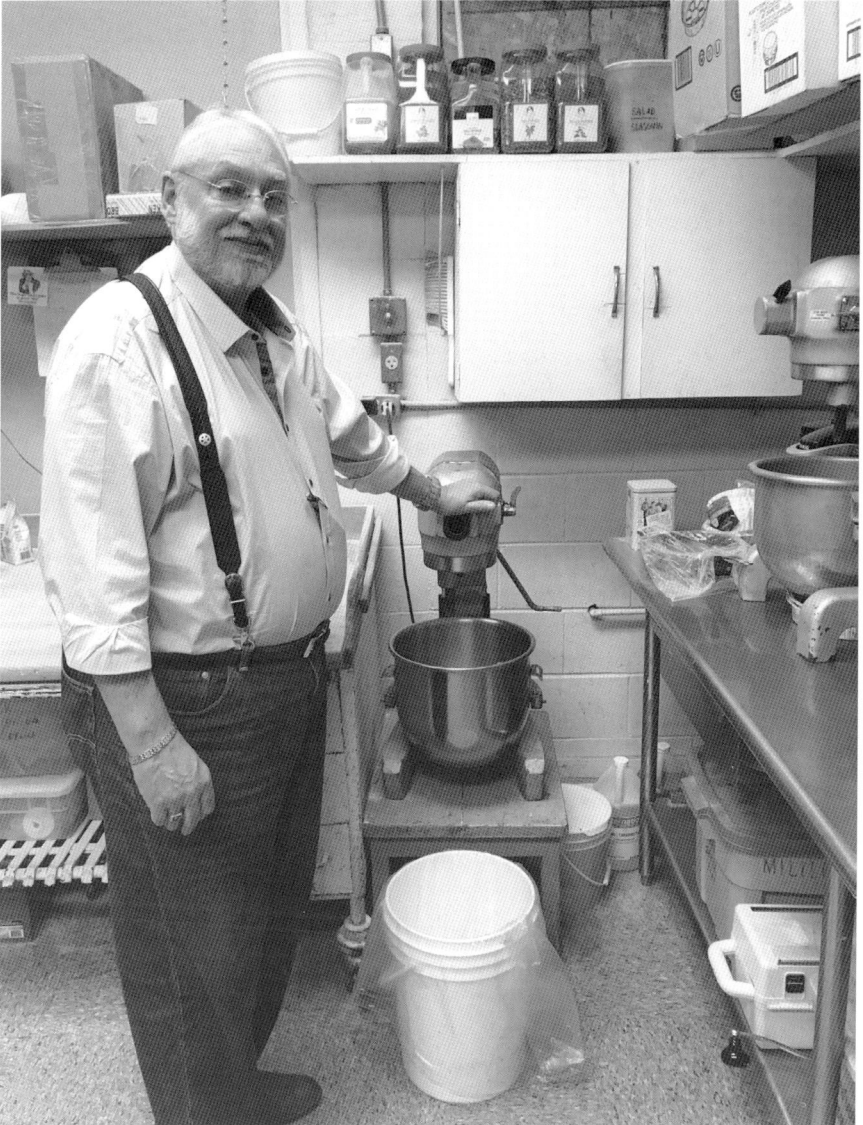

Ron Stout preparing fresh dough at Milillo's Pizza. *Courtesy of Teri Horsley.*

who continue to support us as they have for the past fifty years. I serve kids and their parents today who were the kids and grandkids of families we served at the beginning. They like our product, and we will continue to offer it the way we have for the past half-century.

Clearly, Ron's decision to operate Milillo's in the same way as his father-in-law, Jack, has proven to be a wise one. Milillo's Pizza has a Facebook page dedicated to their history and their customers, and the following is just a small sampling of the comments from those who have supported the Milillo family operations since they first opened:

"It was great when Mom and my uncles opened after the bakery closed. Wow, has it been 50 years? I still love the anchovies'."
—Charles Diefenbacher, family cousin, Hamilton, Ohio

"Love this place! Great food!"
—Joyce Montgomery, Hamilton, Ohio

"Wonderful Place to patron. Food is great as well as the service. If something isn't right, they'll do you right."
—Tim Willis, Hamilton, Ohio

"Congrats to my cousins on their 50 years in business. Our families have a great history in the Hamilton/Fairfield/Butler County area for almost 115 years in the food and beverage industry. Many thanks to the thousands of wonderful customers who have supported all of our businesses over those decades."
—Nick L. Dadabo, Hamilton, Ohio

Yes, the fans and the cousins are still here and still supporting this iconic Hamilton restaurant known as Milillo's Pizza. In fact, the Milillo name is only part of the story of the entire family that has given so much to this region. The Milillos have relatives who also make their living in the pizza business; these relatives are named Dadabo. The Dadabos, as shown in the comments above, are cousins of the Milillos, and in much the same fashion as their relatives, they have operated Chester's Pizza on the other side of Hamilton for decades, allowing them to also remain a significant part of Butler County's culinary landscape.

3

CHESTER'S PIZZA

The year was 1985, and a well-known rock star who was also a licensed pilot flew his own plane into the Greater Cincinnati Airport for a concert at Kings Island Amusement Park. After landing, the pilot/singer knew he needed some work on his plane, so the staff at the airport sent him to get those repairs at Hamilton's Hogan Airfield in Butler County. While waiting for the work to be done, the man needed to pick up some personal items, so one of the Hogan staff members drove him toward K-Mart, then a primary retail anchor along State Route 4. As the two men waited at the traffic light at Route 4 and Bobmeyer Road, the singer/pilot was suddenly overwhelmed by the delicious smell of freshly baked bread. When he asked the driver about the source of that smell, the man pointed to Chester's Pizza, the parking lot of which was just outside their car window. The singer/pilot told the driver to pull into the Chester's lot, and both men got out of the car and went inside. When he saw the huge loaf of the freshly baked bread, the singer/pilot bought one, and after tasting it, he asked the staff if the pizza was just as good. Chester's employees told him yes, so he ordered one, and while it was being baked, the pilot/singer went and picked up his personal items. By the time he returned, the delicious pizza was waiting for him. He ate it right at the counter, and he liked it so much that he asked the Chester's staff if they could handle a large order of forty pizzas to be delivered to his band at Kings Island that night. The staff complied, the pizzas were delivered and a relationship was born. That pilot/rock star was none other than

Jimmy Buffett, who washed down his portion of the pizza with an ice-cold Budweiser. For the next five years, each time Buffett played in Cincinnati, Chester's was his official caterer, and Jimmy Buffett never quite got over his addiction to that pizza and freshly baked Italian bread.

Jimmy Buffett isn't the only one with an affinity for Chester's Pizza. Since it opened in 1954, Chester's has been honored as having Butler County's "Best Pizza" by *Cincinnati Magazine* and the *Journal-News*, and the Ohio House of Representatives honored the restaurant in 2014 for having a history that dated back sixty years. However, despite Chester's longevity as a favorite pizza place, the story of how the restaurant came into being dates back about one hundred years. Nick Dadabo, Chester's son (and the current owner of the restaurant), picked up the story from there:

> *My dad, Chesara Daddabbo, came to the United States from Saint Michael, Bari (Sammichele di Bari), Italy, arriving at Ellis Island in the late teens on a cattle boat. He was only thirteen and arrived with my grandpa, but grandpa had to go back to Italy, leaving my dad to fend for himself. The original plan was for dad to head to Milwaukee, where we had relatives, but the immigration officials sent him instead to Welsh, West Virginia, where he was forced to work in the coal mines. Because the officials at Ellis Island couldn't pronounce "Chesara," they called Dad Jessie, but in West Virginia, Jessie was a name for white men, and my Italian Dad looked like a young John Travolta, so the miners nicknamed him Ches [pronounced "chez"]. After working about four years in the mines, Dad finally made it to Wisconsin, but once there, he got terribly homesick and wanted to return to Italy. Our family in Wisconsin convinced him to go to Cincinnati in spite of the fact that he was still a teenager. So, he bought a motorcycle and rode to Cincinnati, where he got a job working in the produce market, which is where he learned to run a business. Like most Italian immigrants at the time, the desire to take an American name in order to fit in with the culture prompted Chesara—who became Jessie, who became Ches (z)—to change his name permanently to Chester.*

As Chester was growing up in Italy, he did not know that a little girl in his hometown of Saint Michael, Bari, was being raised by a family who also had aspirations to travel to America. As such, Mary Milillo's father, Phil, brought her to Ellis Island on a cattle boat not too many years earlier, and they eventually landed in Cincinnati before moving to Butler County, where Mary worked in her father's bakery on Hamilton's east side. If the story sounds familiar, it's because Phil Milillo was one of the aforementioned Milillo brothers who came to Hamilton with his family, who opened bakeries, grocery stores and, eventually, the aforementioned Milillo's Pizza. Nick Dadabo said the ironic part is that until his parents arrived in America, they never met—despite coming from the same hometown:

My parents were both born in the same town and were baptized in the same church in Italy, yet they never met until one of my dad's relatives in Cincinnati convinced him to come to Hamilton to an Italian wedding at Saint Joseph's Church. They did so because he was lonely and his relatives knew he would meet some friends there. So, Dad went to that wedding and that is where he met my mother. Dad and Mom were eventually married, and he went to work for my grandpa Phil in his bakery, then, after learning the business, Mom and Dad moved back to Cincinnati, where they opened Sunrise Bakery in the 1920s. Mom was instrumental in helping Dad start that business because of her work with my grandfather. In his Hamilton bakery, Grandpa Phil hired German bakers to help out when Mom was young, and she served as their cleanup person. One day, the bakers left for the old Stone Tavern bar around noon and never came back, choosing instead to spend their afternoon drinking beer. After they were gone, a large order came in for bread to be served at Middletown's Manchester Inn, but the bakers refused to come back to work to fill it, and they told Mom to tell the Manchester "no." However, Mom didn't want to lose the money, and unbeknownst to anyone, she had learned how to bake the various breads and cakes, so she filled the order with scratch bread and jelly rolls. After Grandpa learned of her success, he fired the German bakers, and Mom was promoted to her new position, taking over their jobs. It was this experience that allowed her to help Dad start in Cincinnati, and eventually, they worked together to create Chester's Pizza.

Nick Dadabo said that by the early 1930s, his dad, Chester Daddabbo, had shortened their last name to "Dadabo," which the family still uses today. After closing Sunrise Bakery, Chester worked for a short time at the Ford Motor company before moving his family back to Hamilton, where he once again worked at his father-in-law's bakery. However, it wasn't too long after his return that the entrepreneurial bug bit once again, and Chester Dadabo decided to open an outdoor produce stand along State Route 4 near what is now the Hamilton/Fairfield corporation line:

My dad always told the story of how a lot of kids played ball in the field where the market was located and how there was this one man who came from Indiana who always made sure to stop by to purchase their cantaloupes when he was passing through. Dad said he was a friendly, good-looking man who often joined in with the playing children, and Dad said he always enjoyed talking to this man, whom he knew as "John." What Dad didn't know was that John was famous and wanted by the law. As the stories about John began to make headlines, Dad soon realized that it was John Dillinger who enjoyed his produce and he was often spotted around Hamilton and Fairfield when he was running from the police. My parents were shocked to find out that this nice man who liked playing ball with the kids and loved [Dad's] cantaloupes and other products was actually this same man who was also known by the FBI as "Public Enemy Number One." During the short time he visited Dad's market here in Hamilton, John Dillinger never gave my family any trouble, but it wasn't too many months later that he was shot and killed in an alley in Chicago during a standoff with police.

After the outdoor market closed, Chester bought a produce store on Heaton Street in Hamilton, and each year, he sold Christmas trees. Nick Dadabo said one of the first employees his dad hired to unload those trees from the delivery trucks was a young Hamilton kid named Joe Nuxhall. Nuxhall eventually became the youngest pitcher to play professional baseball. Likewise, Nuxhall spent much of his career as a player (and all of his career as an announcer) with the Cincinnati Reds.

In 1945, Chester Dadabo moved his family to the south Hamilton neighborhood known as Lindenwald, and much like his wife's family, the Milillos, he decided to open a grocery store. Chester's Market opened at the corner of Pleasant and Belle Avenues, and he was very successful for a few years until his son was diagnosed with leukemia and died at the age of sixteen. Nick Dadabo said all of his dad's customers gave blood for his brother, and though the community offered much support to his family, Chester was so distraught over the loss of his son that he ended up closing the store. Eventually, Chester Dadabo moved past his intense grief and returned to the food world at the same location, becoming a custom-cut butcher and offering his customers not only a meat market but a produce store and bakery. But times at the new market weren't as successful for Chester as they were in the beginning, and he lost a lot of money this time around, forcing him to attempt, once again, to close his store in 1948:

Dad's regular customers included members of two of Hamilton's prominent families, the Fittons and the Rentschlers. They owned the banks in town, and because of their relationship with Dad, the two families loaned him the money to keep his doors open. Dad eventually paid them back, and his business did not close. About the same time, soldiers who had served a few years before in World War II were being discharged and were coming back to Hamilton as Mom and Dad continued working in the market. Many of these soldiers would stop in and ask them if they knew how to make the pizza that they enjoyed overseas in Italy, where they had served. Soon after, it was rumored that Hamilton leaders were going to build a shopping center on what is now Route 4, so Dad relocated to Dixie (State Route 4) and Minor Avenue, thinking he'd have more traffic there, and he opened Chester's Drive-In Market. In light of the soldiers' request for the pizza that my parents enjoyed in their homeland, Mom and Dad began creating sauces around 1952, and I remember watching them from my high chair as that delicious Chester's pizza sauce was born.

One of the first creations Mary Dadabo came up with as she and her husband sold pizza from their market was the "Half-Baked" pizza, which she cooked for five to six minutes, and after letting it cool, she wrapped it in cellophane so the customer could finish baking it at home. She always included a handwritten note, and the product was so successful that Chester closed the grocery in 1954, devoting his business full-time to pizza. Chester Dadabo was in his late fifties by the time Chester's Pizza opened at the Route 4 and Minor Avenue location, and though his grocery customers tried to talk him out of making the change to being a full-time restaurateur, his decision to take a chance paid off, and the restaurant remains successful today. The popular half-baked pizza, along with a fully-cooked product, is still on the menu, along with fresh-baked Italian breadsticks, steak sandwiches, salads, chicken wings, spaghetti and lasagna. In 1977, two years before Chester Dadabo died, he moved his pizzeria to the back side of his parking lot, and this is the building that still houses the restaurant today.

After Chester died in 1979, his children, including his youngest son, Nick, began helping their mother, Mary, until her death in 1996. It was during these years that Chester's Pizza expanded, and the family opened second and third locations—at State Route 4 in Fairfield (which opened in 1980 and closed in 1996) and at Main and Lawn Avenues in Hamilton (which opened in 1984 and closed in 1990). The main reason Chester's closed their west Hamilton pizzeria was because it was located just a few blocks from Milillo's

Chester's Pizza, Building 2 (1975–2018). *Courtesy of Teri Horsley.*

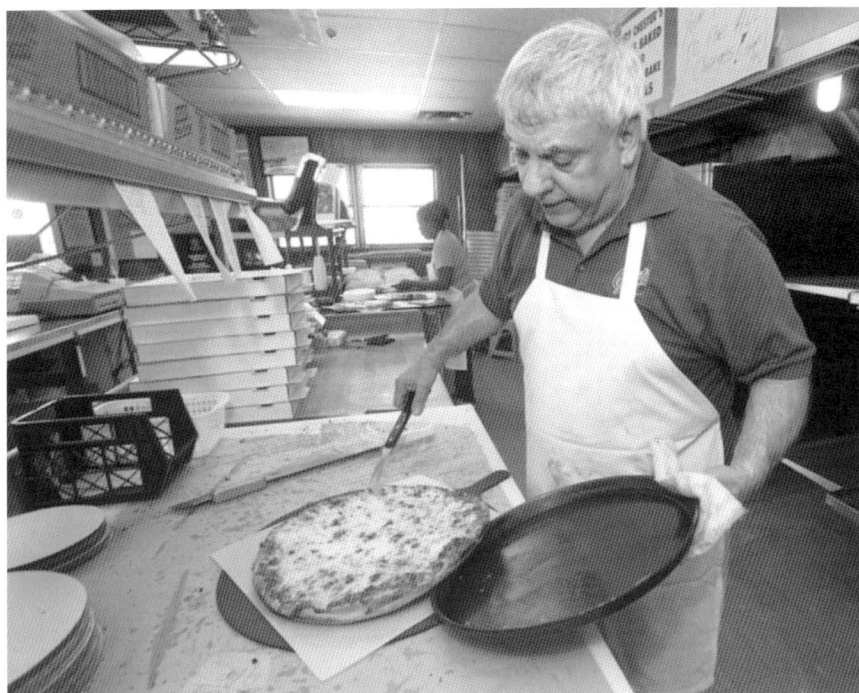

Nick Dadabo preparing a locally famous Chester's pizza. *Courtesy of Nick Dadabo.*

Pizza, which was owned by their cousins. Today, Nick Dadabo continues the family legacy that started so many years ago, and when asked if he ever planned to change the sauce or the original recipe for the sake of progress, he said he would adhere to his father's last wishes, spoken to him shortly before Chester died:

> I remember talking to my dad shortly before he died, and I remember him leaning up from his hospital bed and telling me to be practical when it came to running the business. He said that he understood if things had to change at the restaurant as time went on, and he said to even change the original sauce recipe if that would help sell the product. I was surprised when he said that because of his vow never to change the original homemade sauce that had made Chester's famous. I asked him if he was sure about that changing the sauce decision, and he looked me squarely in the eyes as he said:

> "Yes, change the sauce if you feel you need to do so, but if you do, you take my G--d---ed name off of it!"

> That was my dad, and it was also actually my mom, who we always said raised us with a "kiss and a smack." Obviously, we have never changed the original sauce recipe, and as a result, I'm happy to say that the legacy of Chester and Mary Dadabo, the founders of Chester's Pizza, lives on.

4

ISGRO'S RISTORANTE ITALIANO

We ask not what thou art, if friends we greet thee hand and heart.
If stranger such no longer be, if foe, our love will conquer thee.

THE BEGINNING

This poem summed up, for many, what Isgro's Ristorante Italiano, commonly known as Isgro's, was all about. Printed on the menu, this was essentially the mission statement for the establishment that was considered, at one time, to be the finest in Hamilton. Founded in February 1955 at 309 East Avenue, Isgro's quickly became the place to take family and friends for traditional Italian food, live entertainment and a night of fun. However, the story of Isgro's, as in the case of Hamilton's other Italian immigrant restaurateurs, began in Italy—in this case, in the 1930s in Messina, Sicily, as Felix Isgro decided to head to America in search of a better life. Felix, the patriarch of the family and the eventual founder and owner of the restaurant, brought two things with him to the United States. First, his love of Italian music that left him with aspirations of one day becoming a great musician. Second, his love of good Italian food, which gave him the desire to open a restaurant. After arriving at Ellis Island, Felix stayed in New York, and during the Great Depression, he took a job as a chef at a New York hotel. Though he was poor, he never lost his dream of owning a restaurant, and because of that, his small wage as a chef meant that he chose to leave that job when he was given the opportunity to make more

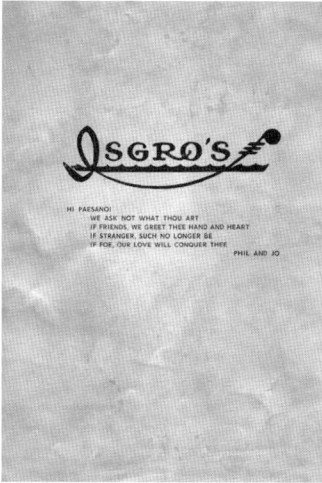

Isgro's menu cover. *Courtesy of Vince Isgro.*

money in Hamilton, Ohio, as a core maker at a foundry. For Felix, more money meant he would move more quickly toward his dream of becoming a restaurateur.

In 1938, Felix Isgro discovered a third dream when he arrived in Hamilton and met (and eventually married) Josephine "Jo" Scrimizzi, the daughter of another prominent local family. They were eventually blessed with two children, their daughter, Marian, and their son, Vince, who later became the well-known organist who played at Isgro's as well as other popular nightspots across the region. By 1944, Felix Isgro's dream of owning a restaurant seemed to be fading due to the high costs of raising a family on a low wage. Despite his lack of success, Felix never lost hope that, one day, he would own either a steak house or a fine-dining restaurant that served the foods of his homeland. For both Felix and Jo, opening a nice restaurant where the citizens of Hamilton could spend a lovely evening at a reasonable price remained a dream that they could not abandon. As a result, later that year, Felix purchased a bar just up the road in the village of New Miami, but after a few months, he sold the bar, because he knew that owning it would not lead him toward his dream of owning a nicer place. After selling his first bar, it was just a couple of years later when Felix bought a nicer bar on High Street in Hamilton, and while it did very well at first, bad luck came once again when, after a few months, his landlord sold the building with the intent of tearing it down, which meant Felix had to close his business and move. Finding himself without a job, Felix returned to work at the foundry, and one summer night, when he and Jo were sitting on the front porch of their home, Felix desperately shared with his wife his feelings of deep depression about the direction his life was taking. Understanding that her husband just needed to follow his dreams, Jo told Felix to try one more time to open a restaurant, because she knew that would make him happy. With his dream rejuvenated by the support of his wife, Felix began searching Hamilton the next day for a location. Finally, in 1955, he found that location on East Avenue. Though the spot wasn't exactly what he envisioned, he decided it would do, but he had to face the reality that he lacked the money to make his dream happen. However, in his refusal

Felix and Jo Isgro serving as best man and maid of honor in a friend's wedding in 1935. *Courtesy of Vince Isgro.*

Copy of original Isgro's promissory note. *Courtesy of Vince Isgro.*

to quit, Felix asked for financial help from his family and friends, and he also took a loan from the bank, ending up with enough revenue to make the East Avenue building his own. It was at this point that Isgro's Ristorante Italiano was born.

Once Felix and Jo Isgro opened their restaurant, it took many months of hard work—combined with Felix's friendliness and Jo's homestyle Italian cooking—before they became a success. But, the crowds did eventually come, and as their clientele grew, the need for more room came with it. As a result, Felix purchased the two adjacent buildings as well as the entire corner of Hamilton's East Avenue and Ludlow Street. It was at this point that Felix's dream was realized, and Isgro's Ristorante Italiano became one of the fanciest nightspots in the region serving great food at a reasonable price. Though Felix did not purchase the steakhouse he desired in the early part of his life, he did place steaks, seafood and other American specialties on Isgro's menu in addition to the Sicilian delicacies that were prepared by his wife. Felix's love of fine dining also found him adding a sophisticated wine list and live entertainment, with the finest domestic and imported vinos readily available for patrons to enjoy.

GREAT FOOD

Your first impression of a restaurant is that moment when you open the door, are greeted by the host or hostess and begin experiencing the sights, sounds, and aromas that make dining out in a great restaurant an adventure rather than merely eating. Isgro's is one of those adventures.

Dining writer Ed Harrison, of the *Journal-News*, got it right back in 1974, when he wrote the above sentences in his column, adding that Isgro's would expand their popular dinner menu by including lunch. Harrison, like most patrons of Isgro's, often stopped in at the restaurant to enjoy what he called "a snack," which consisted of fresh olives and pepperoni, but also like most, he never left the restaurant without enjoying a full-course meal, which might have included spaghetti and meatballs, chicken cacciatore, baked lasagna or ravioli. In fact, these homemade Sicilian dishes enjoyed by Harrison just scratched the surface of Isgro's total menu, and the many specials that were offered kept diners interested and coming back for more.

For about a year, one of those specials came on Tuesday nights, which were known as "Gourmet Nights" at Isgro's, and they found Jo heading up a staff that prepared what they called their "Italian Fiesta" dinner. The huge, multicourse meal consisted of several courses of Italian specialities such as antipasti, deepfried ravioli, minestrone soup, insalata (the Isgro's own special blend of salad)

Isgro's advertisement in the *Journal-News*. *Courtesy of Vince Isgro.*

40

and an entrée choice of linguine alfredo, baked manicotti, boned chicken breasts with prosciutto and cheese or veal and eggplant parmigiana. Italian lemon ice was served between courses to freshen the palate, and dessert always consisted of a dish of spumoni. For an investment of $10.95, diners left happy, full and without a hole in their wallet.

Dinners on the regular menu at Isgro's also reflected Felix's original dream of offering fine Italian food with a few American items also at reasonable prices. Broiled T-Bone steaks were $5.25, shrimp and scallop dinners were $2.50 each and the most expensive pizza came in at $3.25. Even the Italian dishes were offered for those on a budget, with the baked ravioli costing $3, baked lasagna for $3.50 and chicken cacciatore with spaghetti topping out at $4. Even though these figures are reflected in the inflation schedules of days gone by, today, the same meals would only cost around $16 each.

GREAT MUSIC

Great music also drew in the crowds to Isgro's, fulfilling Felix's other original dream of becoming a musician. Live entertainment was offered in the evenings, and well-known local, regional and national musicians were hired, and Isgro's even became the place for celebrities to visit when they came to greater Cincinnati. Patrons included Frank Sinatra, Cincinnati Reds players and political leaders such as Congressman Buzz Lukens. There were also many well-known musicians behind the microphone and instruments, including Les Long, Paul Ritzi, Charlie Cochran and Howard Schlabach. Isgro's even had a "Waldo's Night," paying tribute to Waldo's, another local restaurant owned by family friends. The pianist at Waldo's had played first at Isgro's before relocating to the banks of the Great Miami River. Waldo's Night came after that restaurant closed and was considered a huge success, as the crowd enjoyed many musical memories that had been made at both establishments.

Felix's son, Vince Isgro, along with the well-known John Laduca (Mr. Fantastic), were the stars when it came to playing the restaurant's Wurlitzer organ. Laduca was a California-based musician who ultimately came to Hamilton to play at Isgro's, and he became so popular with his fans that folks would travel hundreds of miles to hear him play. Part of his popularity was due to his playing cover songs complete with over-the-top, organ-based sound effects, and many of Laduca's albums are still available today on

Dinner at Isgro's with (*left to right*) former Hamilton police chief George McNally, Tony Milillo, Ann McNally and Jo Isgro. *Courtesy of Vince Isgro.*

Glenda McGuire and Vince Isgro: music at Isgro's. *Courtesy of Vince Isgro.*

Vince Isgro playing dinner music on Isgro's organ. *Courtesy of Vince Isgro.*

websites like Amazon. Interestingly, it was Laduca who began mentoring Vince Isgro, himself a master of the organ, and it was Laduca who convinced Vince to move to California, where he fulfilled his father's dream by having a successful musical career of his own.

THE END

By the early 1980s, the era of the supper club was coming to an end as American diners were gravitating toward cheap, fast food with fast service. Folks no longer took the time to spend an evening eating a lengthy meal, and most sought entertainment outside of a restaurant's walls. Likewise, Felix and Jo Isgro were nearing retirement age, and in November 1984, they closed the doors of Isgro's for good. Just a couple of years later, in March 1987, Felix Isgro passed away at the age of seventy-five, with his beloved wife, Jo, passing in 2004 at age eighty-four. Today, their son Vince, having returned from California to Hamilton, maintains a Facebook page for the hundreds of Isgro's fans to share memories and photos. The following is a sample of the comments from those who still miss the fun times that were enjoyed at Isgro's Ristorante Italiano:

> *"Great Company, great food, spent many hours there"*
> —Darrell McCroskey, Hamilton, Ohio

Isgro's former location, 2018. *Courtesy of Teri Horsley.*

"Our Favorite!!!"

—Sandy Spadafora, Millville, Ohio

"I remember many special trips here with my Mom & Dad. I was always amazed how my Aunt Dottie (Josephine) B. could remember & know what meal we were going to order before we even said it. MAGICAL. Love and Miss her & ISGROS."

—Linda Pyfrin, McGonigle, Ohio

"One of the best Italian restaurants ever!"

—Donald Limberg, Hamilton, Ohio

"My memories there were the 60s. What a treat"

—Robert Smith, Hamilton, Ohio

GINA'S ITALIAN KITCHEN AND TAVERN

In 2012, Gina Isgro, a niece and cousin of the family who owned Isgro's Ristorante Italiano, began hosting Isgro's Italian night at Ryan's Tavern in Hamilton. Gina was invited to Ryan's because she previously owned

Gina Isgro inside Gina's Italian Kitchen.
Courtesy of Gina Isgro.

her own restaurants around town, although they were more casual in nature, with the atmosphere of a pub. Gina's parents—her mother, Tootsie, and her father, Jack—owned the popular Williamsdale Inn just north of Hamilton from 1966 to 1985, so her experience centered on great food served with top-shelf drinks. While Gina enjoyed bringing a bit of Isgro's history back to life at Ryan's, she eventually decided to once again open her own restaurant, and a couple of years later, what is now Gina's Italian Kitchen and Tavern was born. (Gina's, which first opened on Third Street in Hamilton, is now located on Eaton Avenue in the city).

Though her menu features many dishes that are similar to those inspired by her family connections to the Isgros, Gina said that it was never her intention to try to copy the popular restaurant of days gone by:

> *My mother, like my Aunt Josephine (Jo Isgro), was a Scrimizzi. Though Felix was born in Sicily, Mom and Aunt Jo were born here in the States. While I spent a lot of time with Aunt Jo and I learned some of her recipes, I never tried to copy them or pass them off as the exact ones from Isgro's. In fact, the only thing I serve here at Gina's today that is the same is the salad made with red cabbage, green onions and homemade Italian dressing. While I do serve spaghetti, manicotti and other dishes similar to the ones that were served at Isgro's, I put my own spin on them in spite of Vince telling me, when he visits, that I have too much of this ingredient or that.*

One thing that is similar between Gina's and the restaurant that made her name locally famous is the dedication of her customers. Many eat meals at Gina's several times per week, and one customer even proposed to his wife by placing her diamond in a plate of homemade spaghetti. Likewise, family remains as important to Gina Isgro as it did to her cousins, and both her brother and sister are part of her staff. Just like her cousin Vince, Gina Isgro also runs a Facebook page for her many fans to share their memories:

> *"We enjoyed a delicious dinner with friends there tonight! First time they've been to Gina's. More fans! I've lost count of how many friends we've introduced to your delicious food and friendly atmosphere."*
> —Alicia Gibson, Hamilton, Ohio

> *"Absolutely the best pizza to me. I love this place."*
> —Marci Thomas, Fairfield, Ohio

> *"So Good!!!!!!!"*
> —Joyce Skinner Franchini, Hamilton, Ohio

With both Vince Isgro and his cousin Gina remaining committed to their customers and to their great food, it is obvious that in Hamilton, the name Isgro will never die.

5

SCHIAVONE'S CASA MIA ITALIAN RESTAURANT

As the Milillos, the Dadabos and the Isgros made their mark on the city of Hamilton, Italian families were also starting restaurants just up the road in Middletown. Frank Schiavone II and his wife, Yolanda, were one of those couples, with both having been born in Albany, New York, after their parents arrived from Venice, Italy, in the early twentieth century. The couple also lived in New York and Massachusetts until their early adulthood, not arriving in Middletown until the 1960s, when Frank was transferred here for his job in the retail food business. By 1964, Schiavone had left his career in retail food and bought the Congress Inn in nearby Monroe. However, when his desire for a liquor license was denied by voters in the fall election that year, Schiavone sold the Congress Inn and bought the Associated Collection Bureau in Middletown. Frank Schiavone III, the eldest of Frank II's four sons, said his dad always missed the restaurant business, and he said that, combined with his mother's wonderful cooking skills, made opening their own restaurant the next logical step:

Dad always regretted not continuing in the restaurant business, and my mother was an artist in the kitchen. In the early 1970s, he decided to open Schiavone's in their Tytus Avenue home. Dad was a good friend of Jerry Brown, who managed the local Frisch's restaurant, and when Jerry found out Dad's plans, he often teased him about selling the collection agency to open a restaurant. As a result, Dad insisted that Schiavone's open on April Fool's Day, and per his wishes, the doors were opened on April 1, 1971.

Frank III said his father began the construction on the restaurant by taking a hammer and knocking out part of the wall between the family dining room and kitchen, moving the family's living space to the second floor as his wife made her traditional Italian recipes and served them downstairs:

> *Restaurants are such a personal business and provide such a personal connection between the owners and their customers. Mom would serve ten-course meals on Wednesday nights at Schiavone's, and specials that she taught me to cook as a kid were served. I remember rolling my first meatball, when I was two, as Mom stood me on a chair to work. To this day, I cook my mother's Italian recipes to relax, and one of my favorite dishes to make came from Italy (and Schiavone's menu), which is Pasta Di Pepe (pasta with cheese and pepper). Likewise, I still make spaghetti with garlic and oil, also taught to me by Mom and also a staple on Schiavone's menu. As far as the making of the famous Schiavone's sauce, Mom also instilled in me one very important fact about Italian cooking, which helps explain the secret behind it—she always said that "it's all about the tomato," and for me, it will always be about the tomato.*

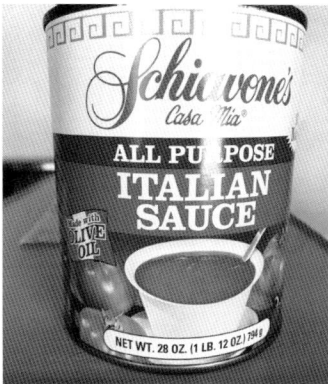

Schiavone's Specialty Sauce that is available in grocery stores. *Courtesy of Teri Horsley.*

It wasn't too long after Schiavone's opened that the restaurant became so popular across the greater Cincinnati and Dayton region that customers began to want to take that sauce home, including many local celebrities such as Reds baseball player Pete Rose and restaurateurs Jeff Ruby and Buddy LaRosa, himself the owner of a popular Italian pizzeria. As a result, in 1974, the Schiavones began to package their homemade sauce, kicking off a successful family retail business—one that took Frank II back to his days in retail food.

The business was so successful that the sauce is still available in grocery stores today. Likewise, Frank Schiavone III said that in those same early years, he took over and ran the restaurant's kitchen for about a year, but he said he kept a huge secret from his father due to a dream that he refused to let go. Frank III, a well-known criminal attorney in greater Cincinnati for the past forty years, said that in spite of his work at the restaurant, he knew he would become a lawyer, as it had been a dream of his since childhood. Finally, in 1975, he decided to head off to law school, a move that his father immensely disliked at first but eventually supported after he came to the conclusion that having a lawyer son would be a plus:

> *I ended up going to law school because I always watched* Perry Mason *on TV as a kid, and I knew that one day I wanted to be a criminal attorney. In spite of that, when I finished my undergraduate program, I worked at Kroger with the intention of planning my career in retail food management just like my father, and meanwhile, dad planned for me to go into the restaurant business with him. When I decided to follow my original dream by heading to law school, my dad was at first not pleased with me, however, Frank Schiavone II was first a businessman and decided that it would be good for his restaurant to have a lawyer in the family. I think he ultimately became very proud of me the first time he saw me win a trial, and though I occasionally came back and helped out in the restaurant, Dad accepted that my heart actually belonged to the field of law.*

Frank II had three other sons who also worked at Schiavone's, and all three also ended up working in the Butler County court system in various capacities. By 1981, Schiavone's restaurant was still going strong, but the Tytus Avenue location became too small to serve the crowds that came each night. Frank Schiavone II thought he needed to relocate the restaurant closer to Interstate 75, thinking he'd draw more customers there from across the region. As such, he opened the new Schiavone's at Franklin Square, a former outdoor shopping area that was located about seven miles away:

> *Dad, at first, was embarrassed about moving to Franklin Square because of his success on Tytus Avenue, but the owners of the mall made him a sweet deal, and he eventually decided that it would be good for regional business to move closer to the highway. His customers always suggested that he do that, which also prompted him to move forward, yet after he made the move, his customers complained that they missed Schiavone's being at my parents' house, so Dad moved the restaurant back to 1904 Tytus Avenue in Middletown.*

Sadly, after much continued success for the next decade, Frank Schiavone II was vacationing in Cape Cod, Massachusetts, in the summer of 1991—along with his wife and his son Frank III and his family—when he had a heart attack. Though he soon returned to good health, the incident eventually led to the patriarch's passing:

We were all in Cape Cod and Dad seemed fine. Oddly, there were hurricane warnings one night that had been posted in Hyannis, and because of the incoming bad weather, Mom and Dad decided to head back to their hotel room, as did my wife and I. I remember watching my parents as they held hands while walking toward their room, and though I wanted to stop them to tell them goodnight one more time, my wife told me to let them be. Later that night, my mom was banging on our door, yelling that Dad had suffered a heart attack. After he stabilized in a local hospital, Dad's cousin took him back to Albany, where most of his family still lived, and after he recuperated, he returned with Mom to Middletown. It wasn't long after Dad returned home that he also seemed to return to good health. One night, he called me wanting me to come to his house for dinner. I was already eating supper with my family and was tired from a long day in court, and I told him I'd stop over to see him the next day. Tragically, Dad died from a second heart attack later that night at the age of 67. I always regretted not going over when he called, but he'd been doing so well, I thought it would be fine. After he died, nine years went by before I ever set foot back in Schiavone's. It was just too painful for me to enter the restaurant.

After the death of Frank Schiavone II, his wife, Yolanda, continued working at the restaurant but was living next door instead of above the kitchen. Schiavone's son Michael then took over the restaurant as his mother was nearing retirement, and he remodeled Schiavone's, upgrading the cocktail lounge built in the 1970s at the family property next door. (A tunnel was added in the early years to allow customers to come from the lounge into the main room of the restaurant.) In 2000, Michael decided to gut the lounge and rebuild the restaurant, and Frank III decided to help out, since he'd been away from Schiavone's for those nine years:

After Dad passed and the nine years between his death and the grand reopening went by, I knew it was time to break out my whites, the uniform I wore when I worked at the restaurant as a kid. I helped out in the kitchen for about three months before going back to full-time work at my law firm.

As Frank Schiavone III and his brother Michael grew older, both knew it was time to bring new family blood into the business. Michael's son

Ethan, a classically trained chef, was given the job to take Schiavone's into the new century, and he added small menu changes and American fare to keep up with the changing demands of the culinary world. By 2013, Yolanda Schiavone, the family matriarch, had survived breast cancer and returned briefly to the restaurant before taking on the role of kitchen consultant. She passed away at age eighty-seven in June 2013. After his grandmother passed, Ethan Schiavone decided to leave to pursue other ventures, and as a result, the doors to Schiavone's were forever closed in 2014. Today, Frank Schiavone III continues to practice law along with his son, Frank IV, and his daughter Natalie Schiavone McDermott is his office manager. Though the demands of the law firm are great, all three of the Schiavones continue to pay homage to the name that made them locally famous. Natalie said that for her part, her father continues to teach her the Schiavone family recipes, although she admits that in some cases, she added her own special touch:

> I remember hand-crushing tomatoes with my grandma when I was a little girl, which made me want to learn her traditional recipes. As a result, Dad taught me to make the family linguine and clam sauce and others. Though Dad still works with me on making the traditional Schiavone's sauce, I have also added my own touches to make the recipe my own.

Likewise, Frank Schiavone IV, a partner with his dad in the law firm, also loves to cook the Schiavone family recipes, and he said his grandma's braciole (Italian beef packets with cheese and sauce) actually kept one of his clients out of jail:

> My grandma didn't know it, but she kept one guy I defended out of jail when the judge told me he'd go easy on my client if I gave him her braciole recipe. I did give him a version, leaving out a couple of her secrets, and my client did not go to jail. I don't know if that's the real reason why, but the judge loved that braciole, and my client apparently benefitted as a result.

Finally, it was Frank III who best summed up the impact of his family's restaurant on Butler County, Ohio. He said that the years of media exposure he received because of the high-profile nature of his work are nothing compared to the exposure he gets because of Schiavone's Casa Mia Italian Restaurant:

After forty years as an attorney, and one who has handled major cases that garnered national attention, I am to this day not known as Frank Schiavone the lawyer. I am primarily known as Frank Schiavone III, the son of Frank II, the owner and founder of Middletown's Schiavone's restaurant.

Frank III is not alone in his plight. Frank Milillo and his family, Nick Dadabo (Chester's) and Vince and Gina Isgro also remain locally notable for the same reason. Their families brought great food from Italy to Butler County, and though decades have passed since it all began, their locally famous names and their iconic restaurants will live forever in the memories of those who enjoyed their amazing Italian food.

PART II

THE SUPPER CLUB ERA

6

BUTLER COUNTY JOINS THE SOCIAL DINING MOVEMENT

THE SUPPER CLUB ARRIVES IN AMERICA

The first supper club in the United States was established in Beverly Hills, California, in the 1930s. Lawrence Frank, a Wisconsin restaurateur who headed west on an extended vacation, opened the club because he wanted the fine California dining to be made available to all social classes. As a result, a new restaurant style was born. Frank's "come one and come all" stance of restaurant ownership became extremely popular with adult members of families in his home state back in the Midwest, and throughout the 1930s and '40s, what became known as the supper club had its "golden age" and forever changed the world of dining out. With the boom of this new style of eatery, the most popular supper clubs thrived in Wisconsin, Minnesota, Michigan, Illinois, Iowa and Ohio.

Supper clubs, by definition, were family-run restaurants that were also run as social clubs, and most of them were set up in a similar fashion. Diners were met by a well-dressed host or hostess at the front door, and after cocktails in the bar, they were led to tables draped in fine linen (usually white or red) cloths, and the evening meal began with the supper club staple, some form of a relish tray (which usually included crackers, carrots, green onions, pickles, radishes and celery) served on a lazy Susan (a rotating tray placed on a table to aid in the serving of food). Entrées were typically affordable and built around American cuisine such as prime rib, steaks, fish, additional seafood, chicken and a variety of vegetables and homemade desserts. "All you can eat" nights were very popular, especially those that centered on Friday night and "all you can eat fish." Hospitality was also key, as the owners tried to ensure a feeling of family and friendship, and after a huge meal, live music and dancing were typically available for customers who wanted to work off the excess calories they consumed. Likewise, an evening at a supper club was considered "destination" dining, and patrons spent their whole night at the restaurant enjoying the casual and relaxed atmosphere.

After World War II, Americans regained much of their livelihood that was lost in the war, and with the return of their discretionary income came the need to socialize. The country's supper clubs filled these needs, and families filled the restaurant seats. In many cases, soldiers who had returned from overseas would drive across the country with their loved ones on road trips to spend their increase in cash, and when it came time to grab a meal, it was the traditional American supper club that often garnered their business. In spite of the socializing that took place in supper clubs, these family-owned restaurants put simple, clean fun first. Since most had unique themes that often defined their intent, the whole point was to promote the idea that anyone—no matter what their income—could enjoy the perks of a classy cocktail, a variety of hors d'oeuvres, a multiple-course meal and live music and dancing for a great evening that would not bankrupt them.

By the end of the 1960s, dining needs in America had changed, and customers no longer wanted to spend an entire evening at one single restaurant. Though many American supper clubs continued to operate, many of them also began to close as fast food and quick service replaced the destination-dining venues of the previous decades.

Today, there are still supper clubs in the United States, but the owners have been forced to adopt a new position around making their restaurants a success. The clubs now gravitate toward folk, rock and hip-hop music instead of the big band and jazz tunes of the past, and microbrews, along with small plates of baked escargot or lamb, are often the highlights of the menu. Technology is also a major player in the supper clubs of today, often providing the music that diners hear. Likewise, family-style dining is no longer the focus; instead, it's about clubbing and bringing the hippest of patrons to this new vision of the supper-club table.

THE SUPPER CLUB ARRIVES IN BUTLER COUNTY

It has been said that many American small towns run about ten years behind the rest of the country when it comes to introducing the newest fads, and Butler County, Ohio, followed that trend with its own supper-club peak. While some smaller clubs began to pop up on the county landscape as early as 1936, most of the area's well-known supper clubs didn't open their doors until after 1950. While the style was the same, with a push for family and hospitality being the focus, Butler County's supper clubs seemed to expand this basic premise by adding huge salad bars and smorgasbords (a buffet with hot and cold dishes, originating in Sweden) to their Americanized menu. In fact, at one time, the largest smorgasbord in the state of Ohio, Hamilton's Eaton Manor, brought customers from across the region.

Likewise, area supper clubs featured their own brand of entertainment. In particular, organ music became popular for those with conservative values and an ear for talent. Millville's Shady Nook became a Midwest hot spot because it housed part of the original WLW Moon River organ, which was the source of the music that was once broadcast nationwide over the station's 500,000 watts.

In Butler County, as in the rest of the country, the supper-club concept began to die out in the 1960s and '70s, as customers wanted faster, cheaper food they could take back to their homes. Though some of the more popular clubs survived into the 1980s and early '90s, their heyday was over about the same time as in the rest of the country, but their presence is still felt. With venues like Nichting's, The Manchester Inn, Eaton Manor, Waldo's and Shady Nook, Butler County has a culinary history filled with successful supper clubs, and their stories of family, friends and well-priced American food are what defined them and put them on the list of iconic restaurants that are still remembered today.

7

NICHTING'S SUPPER CLUB

P rohibition was a dangerous time in Butler County, with many taverns and restaurants allowing bootleggers to run their illegal businesses from within their walls. One such place was originally located on the Miami/Erie Canal on what is now State Route 4 at Heaton Street in Hamilton. The building, originally the home of a low-rent tavern known as Luke's Saloon, eventually became Nichting's Supper Club (commonly known as Nichting's), a restaurant that anchored Hamilton's east side for decades. Proof of the bootlegging trade that went on at the tavern in the early twentieth century came in 1973, when then-owner Elmer Nichting found a whole cache of whiskey behind the walls near his dining room. Nichting's daughter Marlene still has the bottles in her Hamilton home, and she said her dad's discovery convinced him that he made the right decision when he decided to turn his own successful bar into a high-end supper club twenty years after he bought it:

> *Dad drove a beer truck in his early life, and eventually, he and his brother in law bought a bar in east Hamilton. In spite of their success, Dad decided to buy his own bar in 1950, and he moved into what was then called Luke's and opened the doors on July 4 of that year. At first, he called the bar the Holiday Inn, but soon, he realized that there was confusion with the name of a local hotel. Next, he called it Nichting's Holiday Inn, but by the 1960s, he just changed the name to Nichting's Supper Club. Likewise, in spite of being a successful bar owner in the early years, Dad always held on*

to an earlier dream that one day he'd like to own a restaurant. For twenty years, the bar remained very profitable, but Dad wanted to attract a nicer clientele, and that, combined with his dream of becoming a restaurateur and the popularity of other regional supper clubs, led him to open Nichting's in the early 1970s. He always loved the history of the building, and he never denied that it had been an early hang out for bootleggers, and when he found these old bottles behind the stairwell wall, he knew that the rumors about Al Capone hanging out at his building were probably true.

Nichting said that one of her favorite stories that her dad shared from the early years involved a man, a horse and the Butler County Fairgrounds, located across the street:

Dad said there was this guy who used to race horses over at the Fairgrounds when they used to do that there. Though the bar only served soups and sandwiches, the guy liked to come over to Nichting's after he raced to eat a little and drink a lot. One night, he apparently started drinking before he made the trip over to the bar, and after getting drunk at the racetrack, he rode his horse across the street, through the door and into the middle of Nichting's. Dad said everyone got a great laugh out of the incident before he nicely asked the man to take his horse and leave. The man complied, riding the horse back out the very door that he rode through to bring it inside.

In order to avoid future incidents like this, Elmer Nichting implemented a dress code as he shifted his venue from being a bar to being a supper club. Throughout the 1970s, men were required to wear suits and ties for dinner at Nichting's, and if they showed up without the proper attire, they were not allowed in. While Elmer Nichting didn't get quite as specific with his female diners, because his bar business only allowed men, his daughter Marlene said that women were expected to dress appropriately when enjoying one of the restaurant's evening meals:

Eventually, Dad did relax the dress code a bit, but folks still came to the restaurant in nice clothing. You never saw people wearing shorts, halter tops or flip-flops at Nichting's.

When it came to the food, Nichting's was especially known for serving great steaks. With a simple cooking technique developed by Elmer himself, the supper club drew diners from around greater Cincinnati. Marlene said

Whiskey bottles found by Elmer Nichting. *Courtesy of Marlene Nichting.*

the secret to her dad and his employees' delicious steaks came from their placing a simple hot plate on the stove burner when cooking them, cooking the meat first on a burner safe plate before transferring it to the regular tableware. She said her dad would season the meat with a simple blend of salt, pepper, garlic and butter, and with the double process of cooking, the steak sizzled as it arrived for the customer to enjoy. Marlene said Elmer used this procedure on all of Nichting's steaks, including the New York strip, the filet, the T-bone and the porterhouse. Likewise, she said all of the steaks were bought locally in Hamilton, and she said a local butcher was the only one her dad ever used to cut them into their proper size. Like most supper clubs of the time, Elmer Nichting also served fish (Lake Erie perch), other seafood and a variety of relishes, salads and homemade desserts. As time passed, he added dinner specials, and he eventually opened during the afternoon to offer an "early bird special" for lunch. Although there was traditional supper club fare on the menu, Marlene said that what set Nichting's apart from other restaurants in the area was her father's personality, which she said was very big and very kind:

> *Everyone loved to work for Dad, including me. I worked mainly the lunch shift, starting when I was in high school, but it was obvious that every one of his staff loved him because he was such a nice person. He was fair, outgoing and kindhearted, and if an employee needed help, he would help them. He loved Nichting's, he loved his staff and he loved his customers. Likewise, he was a businessperson, and he made sure that each of those cooks knew how to do the food in the way he thought it should be done. If they refused to do it right, Dad would eventually fire them, though he hated to do so. Dad was ultimately in charge of the menu, though Mom (Antonietta "Ann," a member of Hamilton's Russo family) did help out with cooking and greeting diners at the restaurant. Elmer Nichting was definitely in charge, because it was his dream that he turned into a reality, and he wanted the best for his people and his customers.*

Another unique aspect to Nichting's was the decor and dress code that Elmer mandated for his staff. All waitresses were required to wear black skirts or black pants with white tops and black aprons. Likewise, Elmer was particular about his decor, and his favorite color, red, defined the interior of his business:

> *Dad loved red, and Nichting's was very red inside. He had red tablecloths, red carpet and various red knickknacks around the interior, but he combined all of that red with crystal chandeliers and the best furniture and tableware.*

The fine decor, well-appointed staff and wonderful food—combined with Elmer Nichting's personality—helped him achieve his goal of

Field where Nichting's stood, 2018. *Courtesy of Teri Horsley.*

attracting a high-end clientele, and throughout the 1970s and '80s, Nichting's was Hamilton's choice for rehearsal dinners, receptions, birthdays, anniversaries and a variety of special occasions. Likewise, the supper club drew political leaders from around the state, prominent Hamilton businessmen and many well-known local attorneys and judges. On most nights, in typical Butler County supper-club fashion, Nichting's offered live organ music along with dancing. Marlene Nichting explained:

> *Our organ players were Ozzie Kraft and Earl Stagg, and in addition to formal dances, on most nights, we offered music for those diners who wanted to dance and spend their evening with us.*

By 1989, Elmer Nichting was nearing retirement age, and he decided to sell his restaurant to another local family. By this time, the popularity of supper clubs had waned in Butler County, and to accommodate the change in customers' dining habits, the new owners focused on creating a more casual atmosphere while still catering to the Hamilton elite. Eventually, the new owners' family disputes and financial troubles caused Nichting's to fail, and because of these issues, Marlene Nichting said they ended her father's dream in 1995:

> *I'll never forget the restaurant's closing and the eventual decision that was made to tear it down in 2002, the year my mother died. My dad was heartbroken over the loss of Mom, and we all sobbed even harder as we rounded the corner toward St. Stephen's Cemetery (just up the street) to bury my mother. As we passed Nichting's, we saw the bulldozers as they were in the process of tearing the building down. It was awful. My dad buried his wife and he lost what was left of his dream all in the same day. It was just heartbreaking.*

Today, the field where Nichting's once stood remains empty, and Marlene lives just a few doors away in the house where she grew up. Though her father passed away in 2009, her memories of him are happy, yet when it comes to his restaurant, it is clear that those memories are bittersweet. Sadly, Marlene Nichting cannot leave her home without being reminded of the glory days of her family's popular supper club that defined an era in Hamilton. While the building is long gone, Nichting's legacy lives on from the empty lot that remains just down the street.

8

THE MANCHESTER INN
AND CONFERENCE CENTER AND
WALDO'S SUPPER CLUB

THE MANCHESTER INN AND CONFERENCE CENTER

In 1922, a group of Middletown investors raised $600,000 in order to build a five-story, 119-room hotel at 1027 Manchester Avenue. Today, the cost to build a similar facility is around $9.2 million, giving credence to the claims that the Manchester Inn and Conference Center (commonly known as the Manchester) remains an historic icon in this Butler County community. Unfortunately, despite its grandeur, the hotel, which permanently closed in 2015, had a rocky road, changing ownership many times over its eighty-nine-year history. First, it was Armco Steel (later known as AK Steel) taking ownership from the original investors in the mid-twentieth century before selling it to local philanthropist and then–Ohio senator Barry Levey in 1985. Senator Levey bought the hotel to reopen it after it was closed for a few years in the early 1980s.

Later, the senator partnered with an investment company, and the group hired BriLyn, Inc., to manage operations until 1992. It was during the BriLyn years that the popular Manchester dining room again became a local hot spot for anyone who wanted great food in an elegant setting. Elizabeth Kreger worked in what was known as the Manchester Room at the time, and she credited BriLyn with making the restaurant one of the nicest in Butler County:

The Manchester Inn. *Courtesy of Elizabeth Kreger.*

One of the first orders of business was a complete renovation of the hotel lobby, rooms and restaurant. Scott Stacey was general manager at the time, and after a decade of decline, he made the Manchester profitable again. On weekends, one of the most popular attractions in the restaurant was the prime rib buffet, and diners were able to enjoy piano player Charlie Chombs while they ate. Other popular features that drew people to the restaurant were the Sunday brunches, the various holiday buffets and our cinnamon bread with its own secret recipe.

Likewise, Lavern Long, a waitress at the Manchester for over forty-eight years, starting in 1962, told the *Journal-News* in 2011 (when the hotel again closed for a few years) that in its heyday, the Manchester Inn and its dining room drew the biggest celebrities as they passed through the area:

Back when LeSourdesville Lake (a former local amusement park about five miles south of Middletown) was alive with activity and top-notch entertainers like Pat Boone, Dick Clark, the Temptations and the Coasters performed there, they always stayed and ate at the Manchester. For me, working there as long as I did became a way of life, and it was a second home to me.

Both Kreger and Long were joined by the community in their love for the hotel/restaurant, as it brought great prestige to Middletown to have a place that not only drew the aforementioned celebrities but many politicians over the decades. Presidents John F. Kennedy and Ronald Reagan and Soviet leader Leonid Brezhnev all stayed at the Manchester, as did senators, congressmen and candidates for all offices. In fact, then–Alaska governor Sarah Palin and her daughter Bristol spent the night before the governor was introduced by Senator John McCain as his vice-presidential running mate for the fall 2008 presidential campaign. In perhaps the most scathing report of the Manchester's early twenty-first-century decline, Bristol Palin, in her 2011 book, *Not Afraid of Life: My Journey So Far*, discussed the night she spent there with her mother, calling the hotel "raggedy with dated furniture, small rooms, with ugly pink walls and an abundant supply of cockroaches." It was this type of decline that forced the closing of the Manchester once again until 2015 rolled around and an Illinois developer agreed to spend $10 million to renovate it. Sadly, the damages to the building that once served society's elite were so great that the decision was made to instead close it, and by the end of that year, the Manchester Inn and Conference Center, with its regionally famous restaurant, was closed forever. Elizabeth Kreger said the loss of the Manchester still saddens her, especially as she drives by the decaying building today:

To me, the building symbolized the passage of time, and our hearts ache as we drive by it today seeing the deterioration of the building. The Manchester Inn and Conference Center and the Manchester Room restaurant were a thriving central part of Middletown for decades, and now it just symbolizes the end of an era. I am honored to have played a small part in its history. One of my favorite memories came when I was chosen as "employee of the month" in 1998 and given a gift certificate to the restaurant. I had recently given birth to my son and wasn't able to use the dinner out, so the management gave me two prime rib dinners and a loaf of cinnamon bread to take home instead. As a tired new mom, it was the best meal I ever ate—not just because of the food but because of the sentiment that went with it. That is just the way it was for those of us who worked there, and just as in my case, that is the same sentiment that we served to the public with every meal.

Kreger recently started a Facebook page so others could share their memories of the historical Manchester Inn, and from the comments and photos the page has accrued, it's obvious that many current and former patrons share her sentiments about this once magnificent place:

> *"I'm a Miami University graduate. My parents and I stayed and dined at the Inn from 1987-1991. We have such wonderful memories!"*
> —Amy Townsend Manson, Charlotte, North Carolina

> *"We used to go once a month to eat prime rib. Great memories and great food!"*
> —Michael Staggs, Fairfield, Ohio

> *"Senior Prom. I had dinner there and also many class reunions."*
> —Susan Reiko Warren, Middletown, Ohio

WALDO'S SUPPER CLUB

Walter Leihenseder became part of another successful immigration story in the early twentieth century, although he came to the United States from Stuttgart, Germany, as opposed to Italy. After leaving New York's Ellis Island as a young boy in 1911, Walter eventually headed to Cleveland, Ohio, as an adult, where he worked for the F.W. Woolworth Company. Later, Woolworth transferred him to Columbus, where he met his locally-born wife, Viola. Next, the couple moved to Mariemont, a neighborhood in Cincinnati, and like many immigrants who settled there, Walter and Viola eventually decided, in the 1930s, to move just north of the city to Hamilton. Because of Walter's "five-and-dime experience," it was at this point that the couple opened their own store on Main Street, aptly named Walter's Five and Dime. Life was good for the Leihenseders, and they had much success at their store, but despite that success, Walter developed a desire to open a restaurant. According to his granddaughter, Jennifer Bowermaster Rauber, he got the idea for the restaurant's design from a home located in the nearby city of Fairfield. As a result, he decided to move forward because of an available site on the Great Miami River just off of State Route 128:

> *He sold the five-and-dime in 1962 and decided to open a restaurant, with his desired site being right along the river in Hamilton. He always liked*

the style of this one house in Fairfield that was multileveled, and as such, he designed his restaurant in similar fashion, with four levels, putting a reception hall in the basement and a sunken bar on the mid-level with a room off of that bar that was known as "The Patio." The street level included the main dining room, and there was a banquet room on the fourth level of the building that provided meeting space for area service groups like the Kiwanis and Rotary. He decided to call the club Waldo's instead of Walter's, because he thought it would be easier to remember, thus making it stand out. At the time, there was no other restaurant like it in the entire Hamilton area. My grandfather was ahead of his time, as he always thought the city of Hamilton should develop its riverfront. [Plans to do so are just now moving forward in 2018.] *Because of that love of the river, Walter added an outdoor pavilion at Waldo's so that diners could enjoy the beauty of the water below.*

Bowermaster Rauber said the interior of the restaurant also had a wall made from volcanic glass that her grandfather imported, providing further evidence that he wanted an establishment that was high-style. As Butler County supper clubs were still thriving in the early 1960s, Waldo's provided a similar atmosphere with live music and American food. The restaurant featured a smorgasbord, known as "The Board," that typically included comfort food items such as fried chicken, sauerkraut, salads and soups. Likewise, Waldo's always served relish items—again, a popular menu choice for supper clubs across the country—and those relishes typically included potato salad, coleslaw and some sort of lettuce dish. Waldo's regular menu featured steaks, sandwiches and chicken, and while Bowermaster Rauber's grandmother did most of the cooking, she said it was her grandfather who designed and set the menu, which included a full holiday service:

Waldo's was open for all of the holidays, including Easter, Thanksgiving and Christmas. As a kid, I remember my grandma arriving late to our house for our own family holiday dinners because she'd been working since 3:00 a.m. cooking holiday meals for her customers. I remember all of the delicious smells each time my family took me into the restaurant as a kid, and I loved talking to my grandma as she cooked the food while I watched. I also worked in the restaurant when I became old enough, and I filled pitchers of pop as I learned how to cook those delicious recipes.

Bowermaster Rauber said in spite of their long hours and busy schedules, her grandparents always closed Waldo's on typical Sundays because of their belief that it was a day for family and church. Likewise, she said her grandmother always pushed her grandfather to be charitable within the community, and as a result, the couple was always willing to help out anyone whom they deemed as being in need:

> *My grandparents would help anyone, and that is one reason they donated a large part of their space to area service clubs. They wanted to help people. Likewise, there was always a feeling of family at Waldo's, and that was because of my grandparents, as they made sure that everyone always had fun. For my own family, as well as the community, Waldo's was a place where you could bring out-of-town guests whom you wanted to impress, yet it was a comfortable place where everyone felt at home.*

In addition to hosting area service clubs, Waldo's became the restaurant where many regional bridge clubs held card parties. Local women, as well as those from across the region, would travel to Hamilton to play bridge at Waldo's because of the elegance of the restaurant's décor, adding yet another unique twist to the customer base of the Hamilton supper club that seemed to grow more popular with each passing year.

In spite of all of their success, the 1980s found Walter and Viola Leihenseder reaching retirement age at about the same time that the supper club era was coming to its end in Butler County. It was also during this period that Walter was diagnosed with cancer, and in 1986, the forward-thinking businessman succumbed to the disease, and the doors at Waldo's were closed forever. His granddaughter said that people still ask her about the supper club that made her family locally famous, and she said that despite the restaurant being closed, Waldo's remains a popular memory for those who enjoyed the hospitality of the staff, as well as the great food:

> *Everyone loved Waldo's, and I know it's because of the comfort brought about by the homemade food, and the feeling of joy and family that everyone had when they came there.*

With Waldo's perfectly defining the blend of family and elegance that made the supper club great, it is no wonder that the restaurant is still so fondly remembered thirty-two years after it closed.

9

THE EATON MANOR AND SHADY NOOK

THE EATON MANOR

Tragedy struck Hamilton's nightclub—and America's music world—on June 6, 1936, when famed singer Johnny Black died in the parking lot of Club Dardenella, his Dixie Highway speakeasy that would eventually become Hamilton's popular Eaton Manor supper club. Witnesses said that the forty-one-year-old Black got into a fight with a twenty-year-old customer over a quarter left on the bar, and the argument became so heated that the two moved outside. There's disagreement about what happened next, with some saying Black was pushed by the customer and others saying he fell on the step. However it happened, Black fell and hit his head, knocking him unconscious, but he awoke after he was carried back into the club. The next day, however, Black again lost consciousness, and after being rushed to Hamilton's Mercy Hospital, he died two days later from a cerebral hemorrhage.

JOHNNY BLACK

Though Johnny Black's music became even more popular after the dramatic circumstances surrounding his death, his life was equally as dramatic, with Black being recognized as both a musician and an inventor. After reaching his late teens in Hamilton, Black opened a music store and eventually travelled the vaudeville circuit—first with his dad, then as a one-man band. It was during these years that Black wrote his popular 1919 song, "Dardenella," which he later used as the name of his club. (Before taking over, Black worked as a piano player for Bill Huey, the manager of the club that was first known as Shadowland.) Black was a master of several instruments, and as a teenager, on his own, he sold the rights to "Dardenella" for only twenty-five dollars because he needed the money. The song eventually earned over $12 million, which is comparable to $180 million today. Though Black sued those who purchased his song, he only received around $20,000 in damages. Though Black lost out financially, his song continued to grow in popularity, and eventually, Louis Armstrong and Bing Crosby included it in their joint album known as *Bing & Satchmo*. Black also wrote the popular 1915 song "Paper Doll," which never became a hit until the 1940s, when it was recorded by the Mills Brothers. Just like with "Dardenella," the question of the ownership of the rights to "Paper Doll" ended up in court, and Black's first wife won her case after he died, claiming that Black used her song "My Doll" to pen his hit. With all of his troubles, Black began to drink heavily as he played vaudeville, often showing up drunk on stage. By the 1930s, the down-and-out Black had returned to the Hamilton/Fairfield area, where he began playing at various clubs before he rented the building that housed the speakeasy where he would later receive the injuries that led to his death. During this time, Black also began to invent products, as he had when he was a teen, and he was the first to come up with a mail-order product that would get rid of bedbugs; after ordering, the customer would receive two blocks of wood with detailed instructions on how to squash the bugs when they became a problem.

FROM SPEAKEASY TO SUPPER CLUB

About ten years after Johnny Black died, Hamilton businessman Walter Eaton purchased Club Dardenella and renamed it the Eaton Manor, placing a plaque in the parking lot to commemorate Black's death. Likewise, he added Black's story to the back of his menu. However, Eaton wanted to get rid of the bad reputation that his restaurant had when it was a bar, so he joined the supper club movement and made Eaton Manor into a high-end restaurant. In fact, Eaton Manor, which was located on what was once part of the Diesbach estate, quickly became known as one of the finest restaurants in Ohio. By 1950, it housed the only smorgasbord in the state. Later, Marvin Mills, the general manager of the restaurant in 1977, told *Journal-News* writer and local historian Jim Blount that the early smorgasbord of the 1950s featured a huge menu that kept growing in size and popularity:

> *Twenty-five years ago, the smorgasbord became popular, and today it is still popular, with a reservation needed on weekend evenings. Generally, there are thirty to forty items on the salad bar alone, including meaty ingredients like tuna, salmon, ham and turkey, as well as traditional salad bar items like Jell-O dishes, Waldorf salad, relishes, cheese balls, crackers, puddings, several cold vegetable and fruit concoctions and tossed salad.*

The salad bar alone made Eaton Manor unique, as salad bars were just becoming an American restaurant staple when the aforementioned article was written. In addition to the salad bar, the smorgasbord (which was never called a buffet at the Eaton Manor) included a variety of hot entrée items such as ham, prime rib, turkey, fried chicken, spaghetti, baked halibut and a variety of hot vegetable and potato dishes with gravies and dressing. Beverages and desserts were extra, but the entire smorgasbord cost just $5.75 for adults and $3.75 for kids under ten. By the mid-1970s, the restaurant was open for lunch, and as with most supper clubs at the time, Eaton Manor had a separate cocktail lounge where adult couples could enjoy a great meal and evening at a reasonable price. Likewise, the Eaton Manor also attracted the members of area service clubs, including the Lindenwald Kiwanis of Hamilton, whose first-ever meeting was held in one of its banquet rooms in 1953. Today, the Eaton Manor is no more than a memory for those Butler Countians who enjoyed the food, the atmosphere and the hospitality. Its popularity waned in the early 1980s, and the Eaton Manor closed in 1986 before eventually being demolished. Sadly, it is no longer obvious that Ohio's first—and for a time, its only—smorgasbord even existed at 1892 Dixie Highway. Today, the spot is nothing more than an empty field of memories located directly behind a Dunkin' Donuts.

Eaton Manor matchbook cover depicting the original restaurant frontage. *Courtesy of Teri Horsley.*

THE SHADY NOOK RESTAURANT, THE MOON RIVER ORGAN AND STAN TODD

In the 1930s, organ music was popular in America, and Cincinnati's WLW radio did its part to influence that popularity by broadcasting late-night organ music over its then 500,000 watts. Known as the Moon River organ, there are many legendary stories surrounding it, including one about Fats Waller, who supposedly came into the WLW studios one night and began to play his hit, "Ain't Misbehavin.'" Legend has it that the radio station's owner, Powell Crosley, heard Waller's rendition and was so outraged that he fired him, claiming that his music was disrespectful of the Wurlitzer organ that Crosley dedicated to his mother. Eventually, the organ ended up in the Chicago Theater, remaining there until 1960, when it was purchased by veteran organist Stan Todd and stored for several years before he rebuilt it. During those years, Todd also purchased a restaurant at 879 Millville-Oxford Road (US 27) just a few miles south of Oxford, Ohio, in the village of Millville. He called it the Shady Nook Restaurant (commonly known as Shady Nook), and though it somewhat featured the style, the supper club wasn't fancy or typical, and that's why it was popular. Shady Nook became known as a local music venue when Todd installed the organ there, also taking over as the featured organist. Likewise, Todd told the *Hamilton Journal-News* in 1976 that it wasn't the restaurant but the organ that was his pride and joy:

> *It took me two years to rebuild the organ, and in 1970, Rosa Rio, NBC's organist who did radio shows such as Stella, The Shadow and Lorenzo Jones, dedicated it for me. To get the organ up to thirty-four ranks, I got parts from Seattle, Portland, Los Angeles, Chicago, Indiana, Cincinnati, Miami University here in Oxford and Georgia. That's why my silent partner is Cincinnati Gas and Electric, who furnishes the power for my fifty-horsepower blower.*

Though Todd wouldn't tell the *Journal-News* how much he had paid for the organ, he did say that he could have purchased a couple of Rolls-Royces for what it cost him to restore it. Likewise, he said he spent about $1,000 per year for upkeep. In explaining what he meant by the aforementioned "thirty-four ranks," Todd said his Wurlitzer included 2,348 organ pipes, plus all percussions, harp, marimba, glockenspiel, xylophone, cathedral chimes, crash cymbals, kettle drums, bass drums, snare drums, tom-tom, Chinese

WLW Moon River organ inside Shady Nook Restaurant. *Courtesy of Teri Horsley.*

block, castanets, tambourine, triangle, bird whistle, train whistle, boat whistle, gong, burlesque slide rule, claxon horn, doorbell and two pianos, with a solo baby grand taking up part of the stage. In organ jargon, the instrument had four manuels, a double bolster and two sidesaddle bolsters, with the console alone weighing 1,700 pounds and the whole instrument weighing four tons. At Shady Nook, it really was all about the famed Moon River Wurlitzer organ.

Stan Todd rebuilt the organ into one of the finest in America, and it was one of the last theater organs left in the country. As a result, the Shady Nook featured performances by many of the top theatrical organists of the era, such as the previously mentioned Rosa Rio of NBC, as well as Gaylord Carter, Lee Irwin, Ann Leaf and Searle Wright. Todd himself was listed in the "Who's Who in Music" chronicle, as well as being featured in two nationally released titles about theatrical organists. Born in Des Moines,

Iowa, Todd moved with his family to Oxford as a child and began playing performances on the organ before he was out of high school. After serving in the Army in World War II, he toured Europe, playing many organ concerts, before finally arriving back in the United States, where he took a job with Paramount Theaters in New York before eventually deciding to move back to Ohio. When Todd purchased the Shady Nook and bought the remains of the Moon River organ, his future was sealed as the proprietor of one of the most popular restaurants that ever graced the Cincinnati-area landscape.

THE RESTAURANT

Though the main attractions at the Shady Nook were Stan Todd and his Wurlitzer organ, the restaurant itself was very unique. Though the decor was reminiscent of that of a supper club, the food wasn't as fancy as the New York steakhouses of Todd's musical career. Instead, Shady Nook featured comfortable, down-home cuisine and a casual atmosphere. Though one could get a lobster or prime rib, the menu's ground sirloin sandwich, which

Shady Nook's abandoned restaurant site, 2018. *Courtesy of Teri Horsley.*

sold for $1.25, was the more typical choice for diners. Likewise, on Tuesday through Thursday nights, the Shady Nook featured films that were shown during the evening meal, and though the organ was simply used as a backup during the films that were silent, it became the center of the restaurant's entertainment schedule when Todd raised it on a platform from the basement floor into the restaurant, and he and his musical guests played all evening on Friday through Sunday nights. Sadly, as time went on, the supper club and theater organ era faded, and diners no longer enjoyed spending an entire evening at an establishment. Stan Todd died in 1978, and though the club struggled to remain open for almost another twenty years, it was finally closed and abandoned in 2000. Today, the Shady Nook remains in shambles in the spot that made it great. What was left of the Wurlitzer organ was removed years ago, but with the building barely standing and covered in weeds, it's hard to imagine that at one time, it was known across the United States as the "Celebration Place," a moniker that truly described the heyday of the Shady Nook.

PART III

CASUAL AMERICAN FOOD AND POPULAR DINERS

10

LIGHT ON FORMALITY, HEAVY ON COMFORT: CASUAL AMERICAN DINING

THE AMERICAN FAST FOOD FRANCHISE

During the 1940s, '50s and '60s, as supper clubs thrived in America and in Butler County, Ohio, a new type of restaurant began to emerge—namely, the franchise. In 1948, a hot dog stand originally owned by two brothers in Illinois became popular because those brothers switched their menu from hot dogs to hamburgers. Taking their cue from Henry Ford's assembly-line concept, the McDonald brothers began offering the fastest, cheapest food at what came to be known simply as McDonald's, and they hired low-skilled workers to assemble it. By 1954, Ray Kroc, a restaurant equipment salesman, saw the mass potential of McDonald's, so he bought out the brothers, and in so doing, he changed the landscape of American dining. With Kroc's success, fast-food franchises continued to pop up throughout the next thirty years with the birth of Kentucky Fried Chicken, Pizza Hut and Taco Bell. Butler County was no different when it came to franchisees opening their stores on its local landscape, and each of these chains had several locations within the county's borders. Likewise, some lesser-known franchises such as Lum's (founded in Miami Beach, Florida, in 1956, with beer-steamed hot dogs being the feature of its menu) and Carter's (a diner-style hamburger restaurant similar to Frisch's) found their way to Hamilton. But in spite of this trend toward fast food, diners also still enjoyed a sit-down meal that was more casual than the supper clubs and fine-dining establishments of days gone by. As the county's and nation's supper clubs finally faded into oblivion, the United States and Butler County saw the rise of the casual American family-style restaurant.

CASUAL AMERICAN DINING

The casual American family-style restaurant is best defined as any establishment that offers moderately priced entrees with a menu that features a mix of cuisines, often including a signature sauce or dish. The restaurants often provide homestyle comfort food, pizza, barbecue or even healthy choices, and they're described as anything that falls between fine dining and fast food. With the rise of the fast-food franchises and their often high-calorie, high-fat meals, by the 1980s, Americans demanded a return to a style of eatery that included healthier menu choices like salads, as well as places that served more traditional meals with vegetables and lighter desserts. Much like the American diner, which originated around 1920, the casual American restaurant, in its quest for comfort, relaxation and homestyle food, became a second-generation diner of sorts that catered to those who wanted a similar atmosphere and menu.

Today, both types of restaurants remain popular across the country, with the diner now typically offering comfort food and homestyle meals and the casual restaurant typically offering healthier or more unique choices while still featuring a relaxed, casual atmosphere. In Butler County, both styles of restaurants were—and still are—popular, attracting a large number of customers, with old-world diners such as Hyde's and Andy's Restaurant and casual restaurants such as the Hickory Hut and Richard's Pizza offering the meals that, in many cases, kept them in business for well over fifty years.

11

RICHARD'S PIZZA

When a man is on a quest for the perfect slice of pizza, he might have to take matters into his own hands if that pizza isn't readily available. Back in 1955, that's exactly the situation that Richard Underwood found himself in when he drove from Hamilton to Cincinnati in order to get the kind of pizza that he could enjoy:

> *There were very few pizza places in this area when I was a young man, and I had to drive to Cincinnati to get something that wasn't from a chain restaurant and that tasted good. I was young, and I was also looking for a business opportunity, so I decided to open a restaurant that served the best pizza I could come up with. Although I wasn't a chef, I decided to use products for my pizza that were fresh and high-quality. I was also interested in the entire business, not just the cooking side, so though I developed what is now the Richard's Pizza recipe, I also joined a lot of business clubs in Hamilton so I could learn about marketing and running a successful company.*

With his recipe and education intact, Underwood opened Richard's Pizza on Dixie Highway in Hamilton in 1955, then quickly opened a second store on Main and D Streets in 1956. With a continued interest in providing a quality product, Underwood decided to skip the sugar in his pizza sauce, and he did not cook the tomatoes, instead crushing them after they arrived fresh-packed from California. He said the difference between Richard's and other pizzas comes in the care taken by the staff to ensure that it is made the old world way:

> *We take our time to do it right, and though it's more expensive and time-consuming, it is one reason why we are successful. For example, our dough is proofed* [in the most general sense, proofing is a specific rest period which occurs as part of the fermentation process] *for a long time, mainly to add additional flavor into the crust. Our dough sits in buckets for twenty-four hours, and then our dedicated staff punches out the dough balls before letting it sit another twenty-four hours in sealed bags. After the bag expands, we take the dough out on the day we use it, basically allowing for a total of four proofing cycles before it is served.*

Richard Underwood serving at Richard's Pizza in 1958. *Courtesy of Karen Underwood Kramer.*

Richard's Pizza, original location. *Courtesy of Karen Underwood Kramer.*

Underwood said that on his first day in business—October 24, 1955—he made $10.50 in pizza sales, and during the course of his first year on Hamilton's Main Street, he made a total of $2,500 (the equivalent of $23,000 today). In fact, his business on Main Street (a small storefront that, at first, was carry-out only) quickly needed the addition of five booths for diners, as drivers were forced to drop off passengers while they circled the block, because the lines were long, and the parking was nonexistent. Eventually, the Main Street location became so popular that Underwood had to move up the street, where he opened a full-service casual American restaurant that is still located in the same spot today.

Richard Underwood's family said he always put business first, and they said that is another reason he expanded more quickly than some. His daughter Karen Underwood Kramer said her mother, Peggy, always told a story that illustrated her father's determination to succeed. She said that when her parents started dating, they were headed out one New Year's Eve and were both all dressed up to go to a dance. However, instead of attending that dance, duty called, and they ended up spending the holiday working at a very busy Richard's Pizza.

After they were married, Peggy Underwood joined her husband, working in the office, and they eventually had two daughters, Karen and Gayle. As time went along, their daughters also began working for their dad, and they are the two who continue to run Richard's Pizza today. Karen Underwood Kramer said her career at Richard's began at a very young age, even before she left grade school:

> At ten, I was cleaning tables, and I started working behind the counter at fifteen. By the time I was seventeen and a senior in high school, I was promoted to shift manager, and my dad sent me to a management training course at the Hamilton Chamber of Commerce. I was the only one in that class who was a teenaged female, but the experience prepared me for college, and I ended up getting a degree in business, majoring in hotel and restaurant management. I went to school at Michigan State, and I remember Dad came to Detroit and said to me: "If you're going to work in the restaurant business, I have a restaurant, and you can come back home and work for me." I came home after college, and I have been working here ever since.

Karen's sister, Gayle, earned her degree in chemistry from Miami University, and she joined the restaurant staff, now comanaging it with her sister after their dad retired in 1987. While Karen handles the marketing, public relations and staff hiring, Gayle handles the bookkeeping, and with her background in chemistry, she is in charge of product development and figuring out new recipes. Underwood Kramer said her sister works very hard in coming up with the new types of products that their customers want, such as gluten-free crust, vegan cheese and pizza with a cauliflower crust. The girls learned about the importance of expanding their product line from their dad, who, after creating his pizza, developed a popular steak sandwich in the late 1950s. Over the years, the steak sandwich became as popular as the pizza, and today, Richard's ships that sandwich all over the United States, as former Hamiltonians crave that delicious blend of steak, homemade sauce and a choice of toppings such as pickle and onion:

> About twenty-three years ago, we started shipping our steak sandwiches right after Christmas, and I heard about people sending them all over the world. However, we are only allowed to ship them here in the United States, so who knows how they got overseas. We even had a promotion that we

Right: Richard's Pizza menu tasting with friends (*foreground*) Karen Underwood Kramer and Richard Underwood. *Courtesy of Teri Horsley*.

Below: Heart-shaped Richard's pizza for Valentine's Day. *Courtesy of Karen Underwood Kramer*.

called "Where o where has our famous steak sandwich gone?" and had thousands of people contact us to tell us where they were located when they received a shipment of our food. While we don't make a profit on shipping the steak sandwiches, we still do a big holiday promotion each year, because our fans and former clients look forward to their annual treat.

Underwood Kramer said another symbol that is unique to Richard's Pizza is not a food item but the popular Pizza Boy logo created during a family project:

Gayle and I worked together to create a pattern for the logo, and we got her husband to lie on the floor, where we outlined his frame and cut the fabric to make the logo body. We then stitched it together, and Pizza Boy was born.

Though Pizza Boy has transitioned over the years to promote various specials and events, his main shape and look remain the same, making him as iconic in Butler County as the restaurant that he promotes.

With the great food, iconic logo and casual family dining, Richard's Pizza not only survived the changing business climates that occurred over the past sixty-three years, they actually thrived and now have five locations across the area. In the 1990s, they opened seasonal restaurants in the

Richard's Pizza steak sandwich. *Courtesy of Karen Underwood Kramer.*

Richard's Pizza's "Pizza Boy" sending off a shipment of steak sandwiches. *Courtesy of Karen Underwood Kramer.*

Fairfield and Columbia Bowling Lanes, and though those sites are now closed, Gayle Underwood opened a smaller site in Trenton in 2003, and Karen Underwood Kramer opened a full service Richard's Pizza on Nilles Road, in Fairfield, in 2006.

In 2009, Richard's Pizza opened a location in Monroe, and in 2011, they moved the location from Dixie Highway in Hamilton to the corner of Dixie Highway and Bobmeyer Road. Likewise, since 2000, Butler County Fair and local festival attendees get to enjoy Richard's Pizza, as the company purchased concession trucks so that people can enjoy their food while having fun off-site.

Times have changed, and the Underwoods have done their best to accommodate that change by making sure they offer the newest trends in pizza. They have also remained true to the sauce their dad created, and they haven't changed anything about his original steak sandwich. Though they now serve a variety of products, including homemade salads and fudge, the Underwoods recognize that it is still their core product that has kept their business intact. Karen Underwood Kramer said that it is her family's commitment to quality and service that will keep them going for years to come:

> We will keep everything high quality. We will continue to attend restaurant seminars and pizza shows to learn the market, and we'll continue to grow as our customer base demands. However, we do not and will not take shortcuts when creating our recipes, and we don't want to do things easy—we want to do them right. Because of that, we'll continue to build on the success created by my father years ago.

This determination and the continuance of the old-world way of pizza-making are exactly what make Richard's Pizza iconic, as well as locally famous.

12

THE HICKORY HUT

In the mid-twentieth century, Wayne Morgan's family ran a general store in Sallis, Mississippi, and it was there that he learned to butcher meat and sell seafood to local restaurants. As Morgan reached adulthood, he became known as a shrewd businessman, and by 1971, he decided to pursue business opportunities in Cincinnati, Ohio, where he moved with his wife, Lynn. Shortly after arriving in the Queen City, Morgan ventured north of town to Hamilton, and he bought a building located at 433 Millville Avenue, turning it into what would become his popular restaurant, the Hickory Hut. Tully Milders became the general manager at the Hickory Hut not too long after it opened, and he said the restaurant quickly became a popular, casual dining spot that made everyone feel welcome:

> *Everybody felt like the Hickory Hut was home. It wasn't just a restaurant but a place where the customers and staff all felt like family. I had employees who went to work for me in the '70s who stayed with me until we closed in the '90s.*

The Hickory Hut served homemade comfort food, and with his butchering background, Wayne Morgan—and, eventually, his staff—cut their own meats. All foods were made fresh every day, and Milders said that daily homestyle specials kept diners at the Hickory Hut coming back for more:

> *Monday was spaghetti, Tuesday was chicken and livers and Swiss steak, we served the fried chicken along with ham and cabbage on Wednesday,*

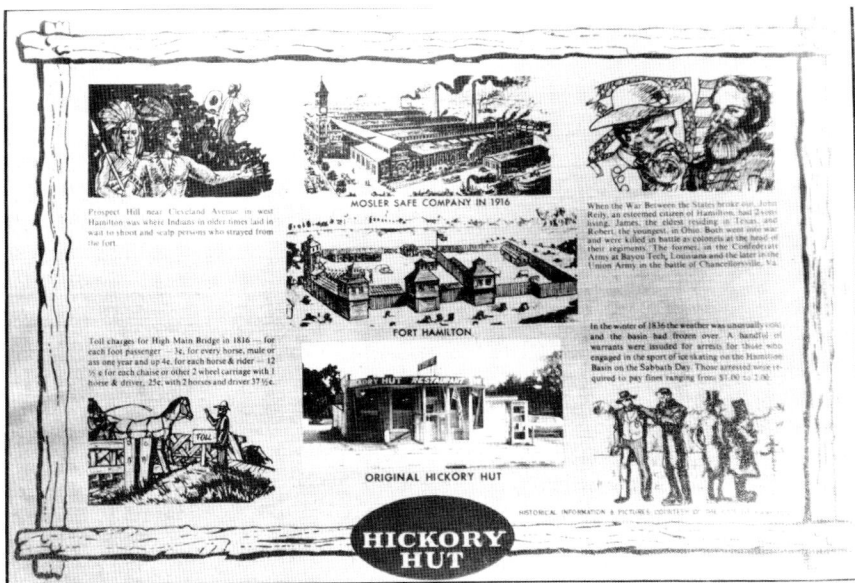

Hickory Hut story on restaurant wall plaque. *Courtesy of Lisa Rankey.*

chicken and dumplins [sic] *and pot roast on Thursday and boiled and fried cod on Friday. On Saturday, city chicken and, once again, pot roast were the specials, and the fried chicken returned to cap things off on Sunday.*

Milders said that all of the Hickory Hut's pies were made fresh every day, with coconut, chocolate, pecan and butterscotch becoming the quick favorites. Each year, Morgan bought grand champion livestock at the Butler County Fair, and he always supported the community by sponsoring a variety of ball teams and special events. Besides the popular comfort food, the Hickory Hut became known in Hamilton as a place where the staff made you feel like family. From 1986 to 1991, Ronda Kramer worked as a hostess at the restaurant, and she said service was not only important, it was mandatory, which meant the customer always came first:

From the moment you walked in those front doors, you had to be satisfied. If someone had a problem, we had to fix it right away. We also had one of the cleanest restaurants in Hamilton, with all booths cleaned top to bottom every day. I credit much of my work ethic and success today to my time as a young woman working at the Hickory Hut, and when I think of it, the restaurant is like my second childhood home.

Name tag and silverware used by Hickory Hut staff. *Courtesy of Lisa Rankey.*

Kramer said that regular customers became so well known to the staff that they didn't even have to take an order. They knew what the customers wanted and would just automatically fix it for them. Skip Weaver worked as a cook from 1982 to 1994, and he said that when he was in the kitchen, he knew the customers by name and automatically knew what they would order:

When the waitresses would come back to the kitchen where I was cooking, they'd say something like: "The Conrads are here," and I would know immediately what to fix, so I would just start cooking.

Tully Milders said that he could still point out where the regulars sat when they dined at the restaurant, adding that some of them came for more than one daily meal:

Some guys would come for breakfast before they went to work, then they would come back for lunch with their coworkers, and then they would bring their wives back for dinner. We had a regular group of people who would come in here three times a day. Likewise, we also had celebrities who ate with us on a regular basis, such as former Cincinnati Bengals offensive tackle Anthony Munoz and former Cincinnati Reds pitcher Joe Nuxhall.

Cindy Boyd Snyder, who worked at the restaurant in the early 1990s, agreed and said that though she was only in high school when she started as a waitress and busser, she became so close with some customers that she still keeps in contact with them today:

> *There was this one couple that came in every Saturday morning, and they sat in the same place at the same time and ordered the same food. I still remain friendly with them, and we are connected on Facebook, often reliving the good times we had at the Hickory Hut.*

By 1988, Wayne Morgan decided to move on, and he sold the Hickory Hut to Jerry Office, one of the founders of the Ponderosa Steakhouse chain. Though the staff tried to keep the same atmosphere in place, Office's chain restaurant experience led him to want to move away from the slow-paced atmosphere that made the Hickory Hut great. Though he kept the doors open for six years after taking over, the iconic Hickory Hut restaurant closed its doors for good in 1994. Recently, a group of former employees started a Hickory Hut Memories page on Facebook, and in the summer of 2018,

Hickory Hut staff apron and badges. *Courtesy of Lisa Rankey.*

they gathered with former employees to remember the special memories of days gone by. The following are just a few of the comments from those who attended the reunion and still miss their favorite Hamilton restaurant, otherwise known as their home away from home:

"I had so much fun seeing my long lost family! It is so amazing how so much time passed and everyone looks great and still stayed the same. Knowing that everyone is still so kind hearted and accepting is amazing. So I have an amazing Hickory Hut family still. I hope we do this again. So far in my life this was the only job that I felt like family. I still tell stories about it after all these years. Wayne was the best boss! He was truly a caring man once you got past a slightly hard exterior. We didn't have much in those days and my car broke down. When he found out I was walking 4 miles to work he loaned me the money to get a new car, and he let me work the money off by cleaning the restaurant after my shift. I am still so appreciative to this day."
—Kim Cummings Campbell, Hamilton, Ohio

"I worked there in 71/72. I cooked there and remember Alberta who made that killer banana pudding. Oh and I loved our corn fritters! I'll always remember the day Wayne tried to make the biscuits only to have a customer get a match in her biscuit!"
—Lori James-Pennington, Hamilton, Ohio

"I worked at The Hickory Hut when I was 14. Started out bussing tables and then I became a cook. I loved that place!"
—Vickie Lynn, Hamilton, Ohio

"I worked there from 1992-1994. It was my Junior and Senior year in high school, and it was (still) a great place to work!"
—Lisa Slone Gebhart, Hamilton, Ohio

The group enjoyed the 2018 reunion so much that they plan to do it every year. Though the restaurant closed more than twenty years ago, it's clear from these stories that the former employees and the patrons who loved the Hickory Hut will continue to keep its name very much alive throughout the Butler County region.

13

THE MEADOWS, ANDY'S RESTAURANT AND HYDE'S

THE MEADOWS

On the south side of Middletown, in the heart of the city's industrial district, a large neon sign points to a restaurant that immediately takes one back to the days when the casual American eatery included the feel of the supper club. The Meadows is located at the other end of that sign, and it became an important part of Middletown's history back in 1934 after being built from the ground up by Mike Mandzak Jr. Over the years, the restaurant catered to local businessmen and their families, especially those who worked across the street in the offices of Armco Steel. The Meadows also attracted some of the country's notorious gangsters, since it sat outside of downtown. Today, photos of those gangsters still line the rustic, wooden interior walls, along with historic prints of Middletown's Sorg Mansion. The mansion, which still sits on the city's west side, is significant to the community, and as such, to the Meadows, because it was built in 1887 by Paul J. Sorg, one of the city's first industrialists. As a result, it remains relevant to the style Mandzak conceived for his restaurant. The Tudor-style restaurant, with its high-backed booths, is still as small as it was in the beginning, with a capacity of just ninety people, and its large, horseshoe-shaped bar takes up much of the space in the dining room.

Located at the intersection of University Boulevard and Yankee Road, the Meadows has long featured family-style comfort food, and in the days of

The 1934 door marker at the Meadows. *Courtesy of Teri Horsley.*

The Meadows, 2018. *Courtesy of Teri Horsley.*

the "executive lunch," Armco executives would conduct business meetings there as they enjoyed that basic menu of soup and sandwiches. One of the more unique features of the time came at the back of the restaurant, where a phone was installed in a back corner booth so the *Journal-News* reporters could call in to break stories as they occurred. The Mandzak family owned the Meadows until 2009, and for years, it remained one of Middletown's most popular restaurants, continuing to cater to Armco (and later to AK Steel) executives and their families while drawing casual diners from across the region. However, when AK Steel moved its offices to nearby West Chester Township in 2007, business dropped sharply at the Meadows, and Mandzak's grandson Mike III closed the doors. The restaurant sat empty until 2011, then closed again until 2014, when its current owners purchased it with the intent of saving this iconic part of Middletown's history. Chef Ken Ledford and bartender Emily Profitt decided to showcase the Meadows' history, keeping the design basically the same while offering upscale food for a contemporary crowd. Chef Ledford himself has an iconic culinary career, having worked at Lebanon's, Golden Lamb, L'Auberge (in the Dayton suburb of Kettering), Refactory Restaurant (in Columbus), Jeff Ruby's and Clovernook Country Club (in Cincinnati). Though the new owners did not return to offering a lunch menu, as was popular in days gone by, the modern dinner menu at the Meadows features high-end cuisine with a casual American feel, such as chicken with raspberry vinegar, southern pork chops and roasted rack of lamb.

ANDY'S RESTAURANT

As the concept of the casual American restaurant continued to grow in popularity in Butler County, in the mid-twentieth century, the popularity of the American diner also remained locally intact. Many of those early eateries have still found success in recent years, including Andy's Restaurant, located on Main Street in Hamilton. Andy's was opened by Andy and Doris Lambros in 1956, after Andy worked at the Homestead, another popular Hamilton diner, located about a mile down the street. Andy's brother Jimmy also joined the staff after returning from the army, and the three of them built a success story unrivaled by many who tried to copy them as the years went along. Before becoming the popular diner that offered Hamiltonians their favorite comfort foods, the restaurant was known as Andy's Dairy Bar

Andy Lambros of Andy's Restaurant. *Courtesy of Mary Jo Lambros Smallwood.*

until about 1961. Mary Jo Lambros Smallwood, the youngest daughter of the restaurant's founder, said her father served dairy products at first, because of a factory that was located near the back of the property:

> *There was a dairy processing company in back of the building that would later become the restaurant. Because of that, Dad first opened Andy's as a place to serve ice cream and milkshakes. However, because of his experience in working for Sam Long at the Homestead, he began to serve sandwiches a few years after the dairy bar opened, and soon after that, he began opening the restaurant at 6:00 a.m. for breakfast, and then served lunch and dinner, not closing until 10:00 at night. On most days, he would come home, take a nap, and then he went back to the restaurant until closing time. It wasn't until my sisters and I came along that he decided to cut hours, and in the mid-1960s, he made the decision to close on Sunday.*

Lambros Smallwood said her parents rented the building from another prominent Hamilton family, the Sanders, who owned the nearby Butler County Lumber Company. She said her parents always credited the Sanders family for the success of Andy's because of their willingness to be fair with the charge for their rent and their support of the diner's business. She said her father, though credited with creating the casual diner menu, actually let his early customers determine what he would serve:

> *Dad was always known in Hamilton for serving a great breakfast, and he brought in his roast beef sandwiches because they were a popular item when he worked at the Homestead. Though he created his own version of the sandwich, he knew his customers would love them, and they did. Another popular item on the early menu was the turkey dinner, and Mom cooked a full Thanksgiving-style meal every Thursday afternoon. The meal included turkey, dressing, mashed potatoes and other vegetables and was prepared fresh.*

Lambros Smallwood said that like her sisters, she began working at Andy's when she was about ten. Her father started each of his three girls off with the job of bussing tables, but Mary Jo said that as the youngest, she was a bit spoiled, and she said her father let her wait tables before she was out of grade school. Likewise, she said many of the customers from those early years dined at Andy's until it closed:

> *I don't think you appreciate being part of something like Andy's when you are a kid, however, until recently, when I came back home to Hamilton to visit, I still saw many of the same customers and their families who ate with us when I was young. Likewise, Andy's customers have traveled the world, with one man even paying tribute to the restaurant when he visited the Great Wall of China.*

Lambros Smallwood said one of the most notable customers was locally born basketball star Kevin Grevey, who became famous for his college career at the University of Kentucky and his NBA career with the Washington Bullets and Milwaukee Bucks:

> *When Kevin Grevey played basketball at Taft* [the local high school, now known as Hamilton High], *he came to Andy's as part of a ritual he had before each game. He insisted on sitting in the same spot, which was at the counter in the second seat. He always ate one of dad's specials, which was the fish and fries, which he credited as being the reason he did so well at his games. One time he didn't get to come to the*

The Lambros family in front of Andy's Restaurant (*left to right*): Jimmy Lambros, Sophia Lambros Vaughn, Andy Lambros and George Lambros. *Courtesy of Mary Jo Lambros Smallwood.*

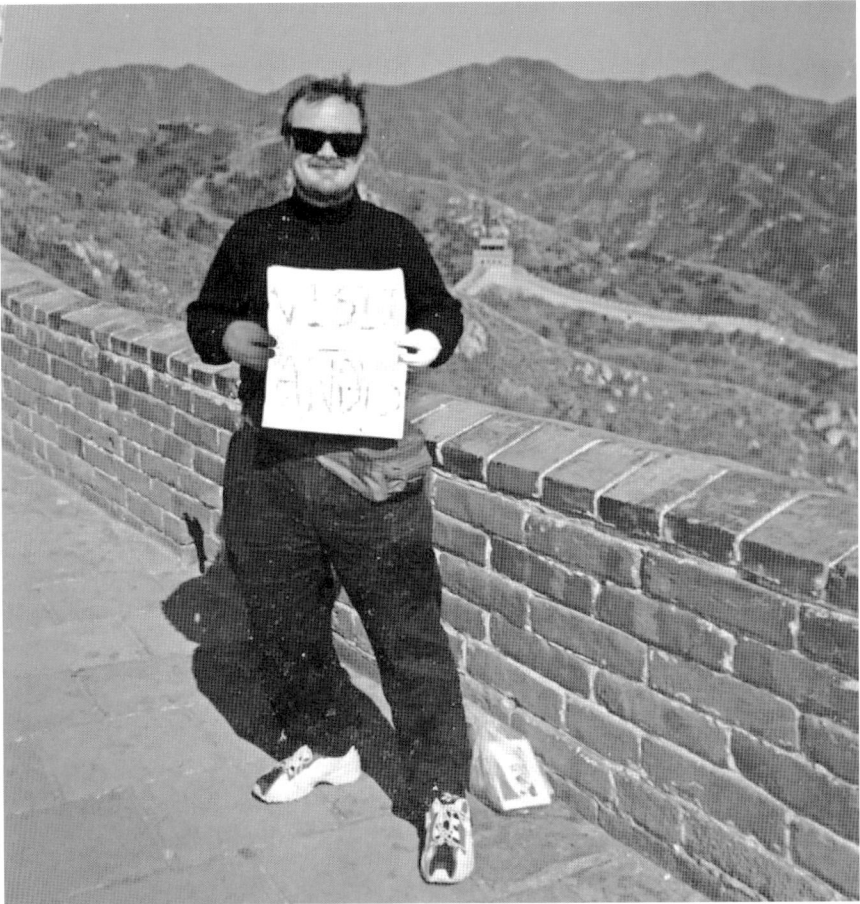

Man paying tribute to Andy's Restaurant on the Great Wall of China. *Courtesy of Mary Jo Lambros Smallwood.*

restaurant before a game, and he had the worst game ever in his high school career. Likewise, he came in one time before a game to continue that ritual, and someone was sitting in his "lucky seat." My dad moved them so that Grevey could enjoy his favorite food before wowing his fans with his ability on the basketball court.

Lambros Smallwood said her father always treated each of his customers as a special guest, and she said that when they came in, he would come out to greet them, or if he was too busy, he would just stand at the kitchen door and wave. In addition to the customers who supported Andy's for decades,

Lambros Smallwood said the staff is also loyal, with one busman having a history that dated back for years:

> One of the men who bussed tables started years ago, when Mike Connaughton, a special education teacher in the school district and the owner of Flub's Dairiette, recommended him to dad as a potential employee. Dad always wanted to help those who had some kind of need, and that man rode his bike to work at Andy's until a few years ago, when he passed away.

Andy Lambros continued to run his restaurant for over forty years, not retiring until 2002, at age eighty-three, leaving his business for health reasons. With Mary Jo and her two sisters working out of town, they were unable to take over their father's legacy, and Andy's was set to close. However, Lambros Smallwood said that in the eleventh hour, former employee Tim Wolf showed up and purchased the restaurant. Until mid-2018, Andy's still served the homestyle comfort food that made it famous, and Lambros Smallwood said her dad taught Tim Wolf some of his recipes when his former employee took over.

Tim Wolf cooking meals at Andy's Restaurant. *Courtesy of Mary Jo Lambros Smallwood.*

Though Andy's no longer opened for dinner, Tim Wolf and his staff continued to open at 6:00 each morning, and they continued to serve breakfast and lunch in the same fashion that made the restaurant a local household name. Sadly, on August 29, 2018, Wolf announced his retirement via Facebook. As a result, September 1, 2018, was the day that Andy's Restaurant ended its sixty-two-year history, and the doors of the popular diner were closed. Many of the Andy's regulars showed up to bid the restaurant goodbye, and many turned to Facebook to say their farewells:

"Andy's was a Hamilton treasure, will surely be missed!"
—Tom Matthews, Hamilton, Ohio

"My favorite place"
—Tom Murphy, Hamilton, Ohio

"Definitely going to miss the place"
—Cheryl Russell Sawyers, Hamilton, Ohio

"Can't believe Andy's is closing! I remember being shocked by all those people fit in there!!"
—Mark Lambros, Pittsburgh, Pennsylvania

"Many good memories,"
—Lisa Poffinbarger, Hamilton, Ohio

"Such great memories, so sad to hear closing,"
—Candace Thornhill, Pittsburgh, Pennsylvania

"Great Place!"
—Kelly Spivey, Hamilton, Ohio

With the demise of Andy's, another piece of Hamilton's restaurant history is now forever etched in the memories of those who enjoyed great food in days gone by.

HYDE'S

In this age of fast food, quick marts and carry out faux food we are proud to foster a family friendly experience featuring "slow" food in a fast world.

This motto on the restaurant website clearly defines the style of food served at another popular Hamilton diner, Hyde's. Founded in 1946, the family-run restaurant features a menu that is typical of the casual American diner that has defined the genre for decades. After World War II, two brothers, Jim and Hub Hyde, left their home in a poor coal-mining town in eastern Kentucky and moved to Hamilton to look for work. They had saved a little money to make the move, but instead of going to work for others, the brothers decided that Hamilton needed an ice cream shop, so they opened one, which soon became the diner that customers still love today.

After making the switch to a casual restaurant, Hyde's quickly became one of the most popular in the area, and as their customer base grew, so did their menu. The original selection of ice cream and hamburgers was refocused to become centered on comfort food such as fried chicken, roast beef, mashed potatoes and fish dinners, and then the staff added the popular homemade pies that still keep customers interested. Hub Hyde kept working at the diner until he became sick and died in 2006, but his son Mick continued to ensure Hyde's success by taking over the restaurant with his daughters Ashley and Amy. With a business model that hasn't changed in over seventy years, the daily specials at Hyde's still feature homestyle favorites such as spaghetti and meatballs on Monday; fried chicken and liver and onion on Tuesday; pork chops and dressing on Wednesday; stuffed peppers on Thursday; fillet of cod, salmon and tilapia on Friday; country style barbecue ribs on Saturday and baked ham and fried chicken on Sunday. In addition, the aforementioned pies are baked fresh every day, and customers are quick to show their affection on a Facebook page set up by the staff:

"Had chicken and dumplings and gonna top it off with this (wonderful) homemade banana cream pie!"
—Michael Aldrige, Cincinnati

"Strawberry rhubarb pie with the little man (her son) Perfection!"
—Jennifer Schurter Davis, Hamilton

"Peanut butter pancakes to start shopping extravaganza day one!"
—Krista Woodward Joseph, Hamilton

"First time for my husband and I, have been wanting to eat there for the past year. It was very busy got our drinks right away. The food was really good, coleslaw wonderful, pie was delicious, and the staff were super friendly. We will definitely be going back — oh and very reasonably priced."
—Tracy Dunigan Thomas, Eaton, Ohio

"The banana cream pie was amazing. We stopped today to get a whole butterscotch pie, and Elise helped me and she was so sweet. I highly recommend Hyde's restaurant for good food, amazing pies."
—Kathy Tillery Hildebrand, Okeana, Ohio

With the casual American diner atmosphere, the comfort food and the popular pies, Hyde's continues to be known as the Hamilton restaurant that treats customers like family. As such, it seems likely that Hyde's will continue to serve local diners for many years to come.

PART IV

ICE CREAM, HOT DOGS AND DRIVE-IN DINING

14

THE ARRIVAL OF THE DRIVE-IN RESTAURANT AND THE CREAMY WHIP

THE BIRTH OF THE DRIVE-IN

Drive-in restaurants are defined as those where one can literally "drive in" for quick service with the option to eat in their car. The first drive-in was founded near Dallas, Texas, in 1921, when Jessie G. Kirby and Dr. Reuben W. Jackson opened Kirby's Texas Pig Stand, a barbecue-themed restaurant with curbside service. Kirby reportedly came up with the idea for in-car dining because he felt Americans were lazy, and he said he wanted to capitalize on those folks who didn't even want to get out of their car to eat. He did so by offering a lot of fanfare to his customers, and when drivers pulled into Kirby's, they were immediately greeted by teenaged boys in white shirts and black bow ties who jogged over to their car, jumped up on the running boards that were popular in the 1920s and took their order, sometimes before the car even came to a stop. It was this practice that led to the creation of the term "carhops," a term still used in the drive-in restaurant industry today. In order to keep the fanfare going, it wasn't long before Kirby replaced the boy carhops with attractive teenaged girls on roller skates, which led to what is now the basic formula for success across the country. That formula consisted of good-looking young people, tasty food, speedy service and automobile-based convenience. Though Kirby's Texas Pig Stand was hugely successful for over eighty years, and its original slogan, "America's Motor Lunch," became as iconic as the restaurant, financial problems forced Kirby's to close after they filed for bankruptcy in late 2006.

Around the same time that Kirby's opened in Texas, A&W Root Beer opened the first of its chain of restaurants in Sacramento, California. Roy W. Allen and Frank Wright began a few years before with a walk-up root beer stand in Lodi, California, but they decided to join the drive-in movement when restaurants like Kirby's began to take off. Using the first initials of their last names, Allen and Wright, A&W Root Beer soon became famous for its frosty mugs, which were kept in the freezer before they were filled and served to customers. By 1926, A&W Root Beer evolved into a franchise business, with each serving hot dogs, hamburgers and French fries along with the drink that made them famous. Later, as the franchises became more widespread, some owners decided they didn't want to be controlled by the company's strict policies, and as a result, drive-ins like Jolly's arrived on the Butler County landscape. With Jolly's and others still remaining true to the successful drive-in formula, it is clear that the pleasure that Americans derive from eating in their cars is still as popular today as it was in the beginning.

THE BIRTH OF THE CREAMY WHIP

America's love for ice cream evolved about the same time as the growing popularity of the drive-in. Though the first ice cream parlor opened in the United States in 1776 in New York City, it was the mid-nineteenth century before technology was developed that led to the mass production of ice cream. By 1904, the ice cream cone was popularized at the World's Fair in St. Louis. After World War II, ice cream became a symbol of American morale in 1945 after the navy built a floating ice cream barge for sailors who were still located in the western Pacific. This first American floating ice cream parlor produced 5,400 gallons of the product per hour, and although soft serve ice cream was created in the previous decade, it was this floating ice cream parlor that set the stage for the development of a faster-service ice cream facility commonly known as the "creamy whip."

Though there is some dispute over who created the original soft serve, Dairy Queen claims to have invented the secret formula that was made in low temperature ice cream machines in 1936. However, Carvel claims to have founded the product after a company ice cream truck broke down in

New York in 1934, and the driver began selling the melting "soft" product from the back of his truck.

Ultimately, the debate over who actually invented soft serve ice cream will likely continue. However, what is certain is that the arrival of soft-serve creamy whips in Butler County started in the mid-twentieth century. As such, family-owned, local creamy whips became successful by providing the popular sweet treats that many of the area's residents still enjoy today.

15

JOLLY'S DRIVE-IN

The story began in Kalamazoo, Michigan, when Norman Schmitt started an A&W root beer franchise while trying to get his nephew Vince to join him in the business. Vince, a young man in his early twenties at the time, decided instead to explore the country by first heading to Lacrosse, Wisconsin. It was there that Vince's wanderlust came to an end after he met and married a local girl named Betty Dugan. Though Vince was now married, his uncle never stopped trying to persuade him to join him in the root beer business, so Vince finally agreed—but with one condition. The two had to search for a new spot so Vince could open a root beer franchise of his own. The year was 1938, and the twenty-three-year old Vince and his uncle took off on a cross-country trip in search of ground on which to build. While driving through Ohio, they ended up at a red light on Erie Highway at Dayton Street in Hamilton, noticing the wide expanse of High Street in front of them and plenty of ground beside them, especially to the east. Without even meaning to do so, Vince Jolivette and his uncle found the spot that would eventually become Jolly's, a spot that still houses the drive-in today. Vince's son Greg, now the proprietor of that east Hamilton Jolly's, picked up the story from there:

> *Before my uncle talked Dad into buying an A&W root beer franchise, Dad worked at a gas station, and Mom was working at a typing company in her hometown of Lacrosse, Wisconsin. After Uncle Norman and Dad found the spot in Hamilton, Dad at first went home to Lacrosse and told Mom*

Jolly's Drive-In's Erie Highway location in Hamilton. *Courtesy of Teri Horsley.*

that he planned to change careers. Based on finding the spot in Hamilton and another one in Gary, Indiana, Dad had to choose where he wanted to start his business. After borrowing $1,000 from Uncle Norman to open the doors, Dad decided that his A&W would be here in Hamilton, because Mom incorrectly thought that Hamilton watches were made here. Mom liked Hamilton watches because her dad, an engineer for the Burlington Railroad, owned one. So in order to keep Mom happy, Dad decided they would move and open their root beer stand in Hamilton. At first, my parents lived in a trailer behind the restaurant, and Dad would be at work while Mom took care of their home. However, if he got busy, Dad rang a bell or pulled on a light on a string that he hooked up between the two structures, notifying Mom that it was time to come help him out.

As the Jolivettes settled in to life in Hamilton, they first made friends with Father Patrick, a priest at nearby St. Stephen Church. Father Patrick felt sorry for the young couple, who lived without a shower in their small trailer, and he would let them use the Fenmont (a Hamilton social club) swimming pool in the early mornings so they could begin their day by freshening up. Likewise, that same trailer sat on the ground of Eagle Woodenware, and the Fritsch family, who owned the property, allowed the Jolivettes to park their trailer there for a very modest fee. Vince and Betty Jolivette worked long hours, and their business thrived. Greg Jolivette said Jolly's became so popular that the couple eventually sold their A&W franchise and named their business after their own:

> *In the 1950s, Mom and Dad were successful to the point that they were able to expand and add a second location at B Street and Park Avenue. In 1968, the city of Hamilton bought that land, forcing my parents to move, so they, in turn, moved to Brookwood Avenue on the city's west side, where that location remains today. By the 1970s, A&W corporate began to be more demanding in their rules for franchisees, including wanting all of their root beer stands to be open year-round. Dad knew that the harsh Ohio winters weren't suitable for year-round drive-in service, so he sold his A&W franchise and changed the name to Jolly's as an offshoot of our last name. Shortly thereafter, he opened the third Jolly's location on Nilles Road, in the city of Fairfield* [a location that has since closed].

In addition to their youngest son, Greg, Vince and Betty Jolivette had four other children—two additional boys and two girls. As their sons grew into adulthood and Vince neared retirement age, each son took over one of the three Jolly's locations. Mike, the oldest, began to manage the Brookwood Avenue Jolly's. Vince Jr., the middle child, took over in Fairfield, despite being a full-time probation officer in the Butler County court system. Greg, the youngest, followed in his father's footsteps, remaining at Erie Highway at Dayton Street. (The two daughters, Mary Fran and Kathleen, were not directly involved in the business). Greg Jolivette said he joined his dad in making the decision to tear down the original Jolly's in 1975, because the old building badly needed modernizing. When he rebuilt Jolly's on the same site, he added the canopies that cars still park beneath today. Sadly, Vince Jolivette Sr. died of a heart attack that same year and never got to see the success that the rebuild would bring. Greg Jolivette said that in spite of the decision to

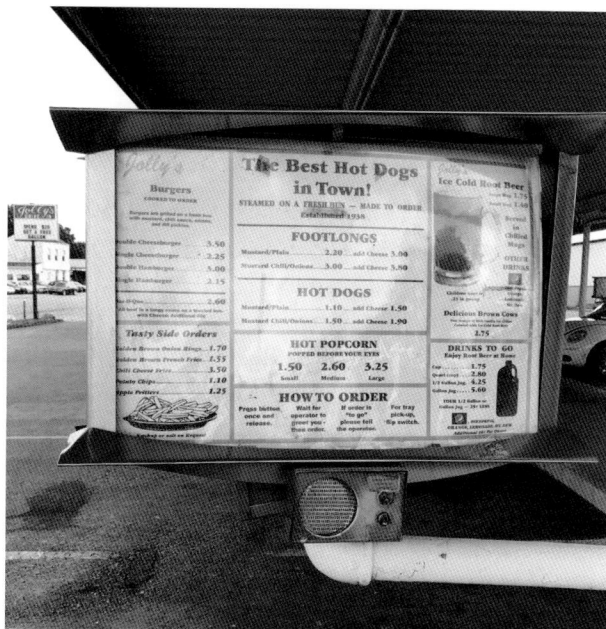

Jolly's menu at the Erie Highway location in Hamilton. *Courtesy of Teri Horsley.*

construct the new building, everything else at Jolly's has remained pretty much the same since it all began:

> *Over the years, we have pretty much kept the same menu of hot dogs and footlongs, hamburgers, fries and barbecue, but we have worked to perfect the chili recipe. Our focus has always been on offering quality and quickness, and though A&W root beer had their own brand, Mike now makes Jolly's root beer over on Brookwood.*

Jolivette also credited much of Jolly's success to the generations of employees who worked for his family. Though each Jolly's location is a totally separate entity, even using different suppliers, Jolivette said he and his brothers have always borrowed product from each other, and he said they all agreed that hiring great employees is the most important factor of their success:

> *I think one of the keys to our longevity comes in the fact that we have three or four generations of the same families who work here.* [Even the author started her working career as a Jolly's carhop in the late 1970s.] *We checked our records and have proof that over the years, several thousand people have worked for us. I had one couple who met when they worked here for me as teens, stayed here into their early adulthood, eventually got*

married, and, because of their long term connection to Jolly's, we actually catered their wedding.

Jolivette also praised the numerous managers who've worked for his family, saying that several came to Jolly's after learning the restaurant business at other area establishments, such as Hyde's Restaurant.

After Vince Jolivette Sr. passed, and his sons began to manage the three Jolly's on their own, his wife, Betty, stayed involved with the business, overseeing the books. As time passed, Greg Jolivette decided to pursue his dream of serving in politics, and he was elected to various offices, including Hamilton City Councilman, Butler County Commissioner and Ohio State Representative:

At first, Mom wasn't too thrilled that I decided to go into politics, but my interest began in college when I attended Loyola University and taught school at Badin High in my early twenties. Mom did change her mind, though, about my decision to get involved in public service, as I continued to manage the Erie Highway Jolly's where she and Dad began their career.

Another interesting side note about Greg Jolivette comes in relation to his in-laws. His brother-in-law, actor George Wendt of *Cheers* fame, has often been spotted at Jolly's over the years and often appeared in the political advertisements that Jolivette used when seeking office.

As for the future of Jolly's, all of the Jolivettes are nearing retirement age, and while the subject of who will take over the family business has come up, Greg's children, in particular, live out of town. Likewise, Vince Jr.'s son Vince Jolivette III lives in Los Angeles, working as a film producer with his partner, actor James Franco. As such, it remains unclear if any of the subsequent generations will keep Jolly's going when the time comes for Greg and his brother Mike to retire. (Vince Jr. retired when the Fairfield Jolly's closed.) No matter what the future is for Jolly's Drive-In, for the time being, it continues to be one of the first signs of spring for those diners who endure the harsh winters in anticipation of their first cheese coney of the year. Because of that, the name Jolivette will forever stand out on the pages of Butler County's history, a point that is well illustrated by the words of a popular proverb printed in the newspaper when Vince Jolivette Sr. passed:

Good men must (eventually) die, but death cannot kill their names.

In the case of the name Jolivette, that is a proverb that certainly rings true.

16

THE JUG

I t has been said that nothing beats the taste of a good burger, and while Jolly's Drive-In offers a locally famous footlong hot dog in Hamilton, the Jug, in Middletown, has long been known for its popular Jugburger. Made with hot-off-the-grill fresh beef, cheese and a recipe that remains Middletown's best kept secret, the Jugburger is responsible for drawing generations of fans, including Conrad Carpenter of Middletown, who began dining there in 1945:

> *It's the taste of it (the burger). You can't get a hamburger that tastes like this hamburger, anyplace.*

Beverly Jones of Middletown agreed with Carpenter, having been a regular customer of the Jug since the early 1970s:

> *They taste more like the hamburgers I would cook at home, and they are the reason why I stop by each week.*

J.T. Maher of Middletown said it best when he talked about the iconic reputation of the Jug, saying that even when people move away from the city, they always go to the Jug when they return home for a visit:

> *It has always been a Middletown landmark (and hopefully it always will be).*

One of the reasons the Jug is considered a Middletown landmark is because it is one of the oldest continuously operating drive-ins in America, with a history that dates back to 1932. It was first opened on South Main Street, in the city, by the former *Middletown Journal-News* publisher Bert Lawler, who wanted to open a restaurant for his wife. By 1939, Lawler decided to expand his business and moved the Jug to Central Avenue, and in 1948, it moved to its current Central Avenue location just up the street. Though Middletown itself has undergone major changes over the years, the Jug is essentially the same as it was in the beginning, with the only exception being the numerous people who owned it. One of the previous owners, who was perhaps the most successful, is Dick Henderson, who purchased it in 1966. Henderson has a background in the food service industry, having worked at the Jug as both a carhop and cook when he was a teen and eventually moving into restaurant management at the Middletown Frisch's when he became an adult:

> *Even after moving into restaurant management, at Frisch's, I always wanted to own the Jug, so I kept my eyes and ears open, and when it became available in the '60s, I bought it. I didn't change the menu, though. I was always afraid to change what made the Jug so successful.*

Henderson said the Jugburger also brought in the crowds during his tenure, and he said the restaurant became so popular that the kids in the area would often tear down the iconic sign posted out front so they could have a souvenir. In one case, they erected it on top of the city's water tower, making sure that the victory of their conquest could be seen by the whole city. Though Henderson would not reveal the secret behind the Jugburger recipe, he said the only negative came in the original from the 1930s, which was made with filler instead of pure ground beef because of the food rationing that occurred during the Depression. When Henderson first took over the Jug, he had a strict policy that only males were allowed to serve as carhops:

> *In the 1940s, it was "the place" in Middletown, and when I took over, it still was popular. Because of that, I decided not to have girls as carhops, because girls serving boys can only cause trouble, and I often had to run kids off, because they had such a good time here that they would linger all evening, which wasn't good for my business.*

Many well-known Middletown community leaders also had their first job at the Jug, and a couple of former employees even held their wedding

Inside the Jug with Donnie and Sarah Osborne, 2018. *Courtesy of Donnie Osborne.*

rehearsal dinners at the restaurant. By 2001, Dick Henderson was ready to retire, and he sold The Jug to John Ridge, a local developer, who sold it to Tom Temple in 2011. Throughout those years, the Jug remained open, but changes to the original menu caused it to lose the popularity that made it an important part of Middletown's history. However, in 2018, Donnie Osborne, himself a former customer of the Jug, who lived in the neighborhood behind the restaurant as a teen, decided that he wanted to revive the place that was such an important part of his own childhood:

> *My friends and I used to climb the fence in the back as kids, so we could come up here from our neighborhood to enjoy a double cheese Jugburger and a milkshake. I worked in the restaurant industry for about three years as an adult, and my wife, Sarah, and I decided to buy it so we could take it back to the way it was when Dick Henderson had it. The first thing I did was recreate Dick's menu, with his help, and we took things like fried pickles off of it, which had been added with no success.*

Dick Henderson, meanwhile, credited Osborne with returning the Jug menu to the way it was in the beginning; however, he said it took a while for Osborne to master the Jugburger's secret recipe:

> *He finally got the burger back to the way it was when I owned it, and that is the stamp of approval for me.*

Osborne said that since returning the menu to its roots, his sales have tripled, and he said it won't be long before he expands the grill, which is becoming too small to meet his customer demand. Likewise, Osborne once again plans to make the Jug a central part of the Middletown community, and though he plans to keep the menu the same, he wants to add a food truck so he can take his delicious Jugburger on the road. Though Dick Henderson is no longer affiliated with the Jug in an official capacity, he still stops in on a regular basis and is given access to the kitchen as if he were still on staff. In spite of the ups and downs brought about by numerous changes in ownership at the Jug, the future looks as bright as it did when Bert Lawler opened it eighty-six years ago. As a result, it is quite possible that the drive-in will remain a Middletown icon and will continue to bring joy to the many diners who still enjoy the delicious Jugburger that made the restaurant a household name.

17

FLUB'S

The idea of unusual jobs really isn't all that unusual when one considers some of the careers for which people get paid. In fact, a 2017 article in *Business Insider* listed the top weirdest jobs in America, including professional mourner, professional cuddler, undercover bridesmaids and dog surfing instructors. While these careers are indeed very much out of the ordinary, Brian Connaughton of Hamilton could also make the unusual list, having had a couple of out-of-the-ordinary jobs of his own as a child. For Connaughton, his strange career began because of his boyish appeal, a cuteness that led him to be known as "thank you boy" and "logo stamper" at Flub's, his father's popular creamy whip:

> *When I was about six, my parents, Mike and Ann, put me to work as the Flub's "thank you boy." Essentially, my job was to sit on the counter; as customers bought our ice cream, I would smile and say, "thank you." That's all I did. Likewise, Dad had me stamping our logo on all ice cream sandwich bags, and he paid me a penny for each bag I stamped. That was the start of my Flub's career: "thank you boy" and "logo stamper."*

Though Connaughton started at Flub's as a small child, he now owns the three Flub's locations as well as the traveling Flubsmobile. Though the ice cream shop has always been a family-centered business, Connaughton said his dad was the ultimate force behind it, opening in May 1965:

My dad was a special education teacher in the Hamilton City School District, and he had summers off. He earned his degree in hotel and restaurant management in college, and after becoming a teacher, he wanted a hobby that tied to his education yet gave him something to do when school was not in session. As a result, he bought Wagonfield's Dairy Bar, and by 1966, he changed it to Flub's Dairi-ette [now simply known as Flub's]. *Mike Connaughton chose the name because Flub was his childhood nickname, deriving from the* Howdy Doody *show. Flub-A-Dub was a puppet on that show, so Dad named the business after him.*

Connaughton said his dad created the sherbet recipe that Flub's customers still love, and while Mike Connaughton began with traditional flavors like orange, he quickly expanded to include more exotic sherbet flavors, such as cantaloupe and watermelon. Brian Connaughton said Flub's made a form of the Dairy Queen Blizzard even before the well-known chain came up with their idea:

We made our Cyclone before DQ had the Blizzard. We started with ten cyclone options when Dad opened, and now, we have forty. We can mix virtually any candy bar a customer wants into our soft-serve ice cream.

Connaughton attributed the long-term success of Flub's to his father's decision to not serve any fried foods, and he said his family also believed in using the best ingredients in all of their ice cream treats:

My dad learned at the beginning that grease and milk don't mix, so we don't fry anything at Flub's. Any kind of grease inside the building will hinder the taste of the ice cream mix. We also use top-of-the-line ingredients, and we keep adding in new combinations. When my parents started, they only had vanilla and chocolate creamy whip ice cream every day and occasionally added in the specials such as the sherbets and banana splits. Today, we make four flavors a day, and after our customers requested it, we added a daily sugar-free option so everyone can enjoy Flub's.

Over the years, teaching school and running Flub's became too much for Mike Connaughton, and in the 1990s, he and his wife planned to sell their popular business. However, to keep Flub's in the family, Brian Connaughton agreed to manage it while still utilizing his horticulture degree in his own separate landscaping business. Sadly, Mike

Left: Flub's Dairi-ette sundae. *Courtesy of Brian Connaughton.*

Right: Inside Flub's Hamilton location—ice cream. *Courtesy of Brian Connaughton.*

Connaughton passed away in April 2004, and as a result, Brian decided to buy Flub's from his mother. While the original location on Hamilton's Eaton Avenue was very successful, Brian Connaughton decided that he would expand Flub's to better support his own family. The first step in that expansion was the opening of the mobile ice cream trailer known around Hamilton as the Flubsmobile, allowing the popular sweets to be served at festivals and the county fair. Next, Connaughton opened a second location in Fairfield in 2006, and in 2012, he moved the original Hamilton location to the lot next door, constructing a larger building and adding drive-through service. Finally, in 2015, Flub's took over the former Ross Creamy Whip in southern Butler County, a location now managed by his wife, Jody:

> *We are a family business, just like we were a family business when my parents ran Flub's. My Uncle Ray managed the business when my father got called to the National Guard, and my brothers and I, along with our various aunts and cousins, always worked at Flub's. Now, my three kids work as well, and my wife is the manager in Ross. That being said, we also have very loyal non-related employees, some of whom have been here over fifteen years. We also have very loyal customers. Some folks come in*

two or three times a week to enjoy Flub's, and for many of my non-related employees, I am their first job, so they, too, have great loyalty to me and my family.

When asked if he still uses the recipes his father created in the beginning, Connaughton said he is committed to keeping the original sherbet recipe, adding that he is only one of five people who know its secret ingredients. Even though he continues to expand the flavors Flub's offers, Connaughton said once created, each successful flavor remains the same year after year:

Though we continue to expand and try to improve our product, we also respect the history of Flub's and what my dad started. Occasionally, we try to bring back a few of the more popular items from the past, and right now, we're thinking of once again offering the pointed sundae cone, a pointed cake cone with fudge and ice cream inside and a cherry on top. My dad created it fifty years ago, but it went away in the '80s. Now, we're going to bring it back because one of my managers who worked for my parents as a kid remembered it and thinks it will once again be a big seller.

Though Connaughton continues to expand his flavors while bringing Flub's to other communities around Butler County, he still has plans for expansion, with an ultimate goal of having five Flub's locations within the next several years. When asked about Flub's popularity and his thoughts about why the ice cream shop remains an important part of Butler County's culinary history, Connaughton said that even though quality, service and loyalty are important, it ultimately boils down to the fact that Flub's spreads good cheer:

When you're coming to Flub's to get ice cream, you're happy. Likewise, the kid who is waiting on you is happy, and whether you're two or one hundred and two, ice cream probably makes you happy, so with all of this happiness, Flub's continues to be a success.

If there is any doubt about Connaughton's point about the importance of joy, the long lines around Flub's on any given summer day prove that he indeed is correct.

18

THE CONE

I t isn't often that a local barber decides to become the owner of a creamy whip only to later be joined in that business by his insurance-agent son. However, in the case of the Cone in West Chester Township, current owner Keith Wren said that is exactly the way the history played out:

> *My parents started the Cone in 1974, when I was fourteen. They purchased K&W Creamy Whip, which was on the border between Lockland and Reading on Wyoming Avenue, in Cincinnati. My dad, Kenneth, was a barber next door to K&W, yet for whatever reason, he always wanted to own an ice cream shop. Dad, along with my mom, Louella, thought the creamy whip was in a good location, so they bought it, and what would later become the Cone was born.*

After twenty years of success in Lockland, the Wrens decided to move their creamy whip to 6855 Tylersville Road, in West Chester Township, in 1995. They did so because they lived in the Butler County community, and their son Keith owned an insurance agency there, and he was willing to join them in business if they moved. Kenneth Wren planned to call the new store K&W II, but Keith's wife, Valerie, said it should be called the Cone, so the family changed the business's name. One of the biggest differences between the Wrens and other small business owners in the area is their flair for the dramatic. In the case of the Cone, both father and son decided that the building should be shaped like a large ice cream cone, which—in and of itself—makes the Cone iconic:

My dad and I decided we wanted to build something unique when they moved to West Chester, so we went to Florida, where we knew a man who made cone-shaped buildings to sell to companies who, in turn, sold soft serve ice cream. When we arrived in Florida, there were buildings that were lying in pieces, and those pieces were stretched and warped due to the high Florida humidity. However, my wife's father was a talented builder, so we bought those warped pieces of building, and he worked with us to construct the Cone as you see it today. We actually built the building in late 1994, because we knew my parents were going to move to West Chester in '95. The township trustees tried to stop our building it because it so clearly advertised our product, but after spending $35,000 to construct the Cone, we fought the township and won.

After the Wrens opened, they eventually added a dining room, a game room, kiddie rides and a drive-through at the small structure. Kenneth Wren also wanted to add vintage pinball machines to that game room, because during the 1990s, when he was in his seventies, he was crowned the World Champion of Pinball in the league in which he competed:

Many of these vintage pinball machines were from my dad's collection, and we attract "kids of all ages" who enjoy playing on them. Likewise, when we added the drive-through, we were quick to realize that it is probably the longest-standing drive-through in the state of Ohio.

Keith Wren's parents retired from the business in the early 2000s, and he took over the management of the Cone before finally buying it in 2016. One of the first changes he made when taking over was to remove most of the fried foods from the menu, choosing instead to focus on his core product. Wren is good friends with Brian Connaughton, the owner of all of the Flub's creamy whips, and though the two are technically competitors, they are located in different parts of the county, and as such, they often help each other, especially in product development:

A funny story in regards to how competitors can also be friends and help each other. A few years ago, Flub's served peanut butter ice cream, and I served pumpkin. I really wanted to serve Flub's peanut butter at the Cone, and Brian wanted to serve my pumpkin at Flub's. So, based on those desires, we switched, with me happily giving the pumpkin recipe to him, and in return, he gave the peanut butter recipe to me. Our two families have been friends since our parents ran the businesses, and we continue to be friends as well.

Left: Keith Wren, owner of the Cone in West Chester Township. *Courtesy of Keith Wren.*

Right: Crowds enjoying a trip to the Cone in West Chester Township. *Courtesy of Keith Wren.*

Wren said that just as Mike Connaughton did for Flub's in the beginning, his father, Kenneth, created the orange sherbet recipe that is still used at the Cone today.

> *My dad worked with a Cincinnati food chemist to create our orange sherbet, and we own the rights to the specific recipe, which is all natural, delicious and can only be bought here. We also offer key lime, blue raspberry and pink lemonade Italian ices, which are dairy-free, and my strawberry ice cream is made fresh with real fruit. That being said, we once again worked with Brian Connaughton, who helped us develop our pineapple sherbet recipe.*

Wren said his goal when creating all of these sweet treats was to create a place where families could have a good time while enjoying a good product in the atmosphere of an old-fashioned ice cream parlor. In the early 2000s, he added cakes and pies, and in the 2010s, he introduced raw cookie dough to his product line. Since the start of the twenty-first century, he added mobile Cones, which are mobile trailers used at area festivals. In light of all

Iconic pinball machines at the Cone. *Courtesy of Keith Wren.*

Left: Lion's-head drinking fountain at the Cone. *Courtesy of Keith Wren.*

Right: The Cone with ice cream statue. *Courtesy of Keith Wren.*

of this innovation, the Cone has been the subject of much local—and even some national—attention:

> *PBS did a half-hour documentary featuring the Cone, as we were listed in the film as one of the top ten iconic places to visit in Cincinnati. Likewise, we were featured on A&E, and it is my hope that we'll eventually be featured on the Food Network because of what we do. The reason we're featured on these national broadcasts is that no one can say they have what we have here. We have an unusual building, vintage pinball machines as part of a complete game room and fresh product made with all-natural ingredients. I have people come here all of the time who have been coming here for years. I even started selling doggie cups to their dogs, which include peanut butter and vanilla ice cream with a dog biscuit. When we decided all those years ago to build the Cone here in West Chester, we wanted to offer the best soft serve in the area, and we wanted our look to be recognizable and iconic.*

Based on the past, present and likely future popularity of the Cone, it is apparent that Wren's goal of becoming an "iconic" restaurant has clearly been achieved.

EPILOGUE

Defining the word "iconic" is a difficult process when considering the favorite restaurants located in a large area such as Butler County, Ohio. While some—such as Milillo's, Chester's, Nichting's and Isgro's—have to be included on such an iconic list because everyone considers them to be so, others are a bit more obscure, or there just isn't much information available about these restaurants' pasts. But that doesn't mean these restaurants weren't important to those who enjoyed them or to the culinary history of our diverse Midwestern food culture. With that in mind, I wanted to pay brief tribute to the restaurants with stories that are not fully shared in this book but easily could have been included if space and time allowed:

AUNT BEE'S HOME COOKING: Opened at 3222 Dixie Highway in Fairfield in 1975. Served homestyle food with biscuits and gravy featured daily starting at 6:00 a.m.

BILL KNAPPS: Another favorite that was part of a national chain. Located on Main Street in Hamilton, the restaurant drew the after-church crowd. Popular for dessert, including its locally famous cinnamon ice cream.

BREWERS COFFEE SHOP: Formerly located at 750 East Avenue in Hamilton. Customers said they felt like family and appreciated being served breakfast any time of day. Traditional American diner-style food.

Three fires in five years—with the last one occurring in 2013—led to its closing a few years later.

CAPOZZI'S: A popular Italian restaurant on Central Avenue in Middletown. Known for its Wednesday night spaghetti special and casual dining and bar area, the restaurant closed in 2007, although its popular sauce is still available in grocery stores.

CARTER'S: West Hamilton had a Carter's Drive-In in the late 1950s and early 1960s. An advertisement in the *Hamilton Journal-News* in 1960 cited Carter's as being famous for homemade pies, thick malts and big burgers. The national chain restaurant was similar to Frisch's, which is still located throughout greater Cincinnati.

CHINESE LANTERN: Closed in 2017 after a thirty-year run in Hamilton. Located at 965 Main Street, the restaurant's owners, Sherry and Peter Chung, closed it after deciding to retire. The restaurant reopened under new ownership in early 2018 with a new name—Asian Lantern.

DIXIE HAMBURGERS: A Lindenwald (Hamilton neighborhood) classic for much of the late twentieth century. The burgers, similar to those served at White Castle, were known affectionately as belly bombers. In addition to the lunch crowd, the restaurant drew late-night customers who often needed to partake in their small beef patty, grilled with onions, and one pickle on a lightly toasted bun after a night of heavy partying. It was located on State Route 4 (Dixie Highway). One of the owners of Dixie Hamburgers said he couldn't stand the smell of his product in spite of their popularity, claiming that to him, they smelled like "dead goat."

KOSTAS RESTAURANT: Located at 221 Court Street in Hamilton. The small diner has long catered to the downtown business and legal crowds, as it sits near the county courts. Diner-style American food featuring homestyle meals and daily specials. A strong 1950s vibe, and reasonably priced.

LAKESIDE INN: One of Middletown's oldest restaurants. It opened in 1921, and the eighth owner, Jimmy Valentine, closed it in 2011 due to financial troubles. Located at 2019 Tytus Avenue, the restaurant was primarily a bar but was also known for its Friday fish dinners and sandwiches and fries for lunch. Likewise, in the 2010s, prime rib was served every night. The restaurant went into foreclosure in September 2011 and was auctioned off at the end of that year. Interestingly, the bar/restaurant did not sit beside a lake.

THE LIBERTY RESTAURANT: Located at 1212 Central Avenue in Middletown. The Liberty, first owned by Butler County common pleas judge Anthony Valen, featured a diner atmosphere with homestyle food. Judge Valen, the son of Greek immigrants, considered owning The Liberty to be one of his greatest accomplishments during his distinguished career. Judge Valen passed away in 2014, and the Liberty closed soon afterward.

LUM'S: A national chain based in Florida but with an east Hamilton location in the 1970s. Famous for beer-steamed hot dogs and homestyle daily specials.

THE MILLVILLE RESTAURANT: Located at 1198 Ross Millville Road in the village of Millville, the small diner that serves homestyle comfort food is jokingly known to locals as the Millville Maisonette (a former five-star, *Mobil Travel Guide*–rated French restaurant in Cincinnati). The Millville Restaurant serves breakfast and lunch starting at 5:30 a.m. It caters to Butler County sheriff's deputies who have to work first shift.

PUSCH'S FAMILY RESTAURANT: Formerly located at 945 Nilles Road in Fairfield, Pusch's served American food and had a reputation for great pancakes. Likewise, homey favorites such as meatloaf, open-faced roast beef sandwiches and chicken drew comfort-food fans, and breakfast was served all day. Pusch's closed in 2002.

THE RAINBOW GARDENS: This popular supper club in the village of Millville offered great seafood, had a small dance floor and served its specialty homemade Thousand Island dressing in the 1950s, '60s and '70s. With a reputation for being a stag bar, The Rainbow Gardens conducted an advertising campaign in 1955 that assured local residents that families were welcome.

RED'S HAMBURGERS: Located on Riverside Drive in New Miami, this was another White Castle–style hamburger joint. Red's served comfort food, although it remained all about the hamburger and fries. The name Red's was changed to Mel's in 2016.

VENICE CASTLE: Located at the intersection of Cincinnati Brookville and Hamilton Cleves Roads in Ross, the building that housed the casual restaurant and bar was constructed in 1840. Known for having what some called "the best roast beef sandwich in Butler County," the restaurant fell into disrepair in 2015 and was soon closed and demolished.

WOLPERTS CAFÉ: Formerly located at 1005 Eaton Avenue in Hamilton, the popular bar served sandwiches along with beer and top-shelf liquor. The restaurant closed in 2010, and the building now houses Gina's Italian Kitchen and Tavern.

NOTE FROM THE AUTHOR

When I was determining which restaurants to include in this book, I used a five-pronged system to define what I believed to be an "iconic" restaurant. First, I had to personally consider them "iconic," meaning that I spent quite a bit of time in each of them in my personal life and in my former career as a restaurant critic. Likewise, I determined that chains would not be featured unless they originated in Butler County, Ohio. Next, there had to be enough available information about those included, which would allow me to dig into the history and stories behind what made them great. Likewise, I found it important to include some restaurants that are still in business today, illustrating what it takes to remain successful—in some cases, for over one hundred years. Finally, I surveyed friends and colleagues and included what they, too, thought should be deemed iconic, which added to the overall list. With the limited space in this book, I decided to only include restaurants with a history dating to the second half of the twentieth century due to the sheer volume of great restaurants in this region.

This book was also compiled from many interviews with the various families involved with the restaurants listed. As such, the author recognizes that individual memories can sometimes fade, and in light of that, she bears no liability for any of the information presented here. Likewise, all photos chosen for publication met required standards; the omission of any provided photos simply occurred because the quality was below what is acceptable to the publisher.

BIBLIOGRAPHY

A&W Root Beer. "Our History." Accessed August, 27, 2018. http://www. awrootbeer.com.

Advertisement for Aunt Bee's Home Cooking. *Journal-News*, May 13, 1975. Accessed August 28, 2018. http://www.newspaperarchive.com.

Advertisement for Carter's Restaurant. *Journal-News*, 1960. Accessed August 28, 2018. http://www.google.com.

AK Steel. "About Us." Accessed August 7, 2018. http://www.aksteel.com.

Blount, Jim. "Eaton Manor's Smorgasbord Begins with 38 Items on the Salad Bar." *Journal-News*, February 3, 1977. Accessed August 19, 2018. http://www.newspapers.com.

Buckholtz, Sarah. "The History of Supper Clubs: Bringing Families Together for Dinner." *Antique Archaeology*, October 19, 2016. Accessed August 12, 2018. http://www.antiquearchaeology.com.

Callahan, Denise G. "Restaurant Graveyard, Venice Castle." Accessed August, 28, 2018. http://www.restaurantgraveyard.com.

Campbell, Polly. "How One Small Village Shaped Italian Culture in the Queen City." Cincinnati.com, March 2, 2017. Accessed August 7, 2018. http://www.cincinnati.com.

Centralia Daisies. "The Wonderful World of Wurlitzer and The Happy Hammond." October 18, 2011. Accessed August 16, 2018. http://www. centraliadaisies.com

Cincinnati.Bites. "Pusch's Family Restaurant." Accessed August 28, 2018. http://www.cincinnatibites.com.

Club Dardanella. "The History of Eaton Manor." Accessed August 19, 2018. http://www.sites.google.com/a/lanepl.org/butler/home.

Connaughton, Brian. Interview with author conducted June 20, 2018.

Currency Conversions. "Dollar Times Converter." Accessed August 14, 2018. http://www.dollartimes.com.

Dadabo, Nick. Interview with author conducted June 11, 2018.

———. "Jimmy Buffett and Chester's Pizza." Facebook. Accessed August 21, 2018. http://www.facebook.com.

Ecreamery. "The History of Ice Cream in America." *New York Times*, June 22, 1958. Accessed August 22, 2018. http://www.newspapers.com.

Essex Organ Museum. "John LaDuca." Accessed August 21, 2018. http://www.essexorganmuseum.com.

Facebook. "Public commentary about Andy's Restaurant." Accessed September 1, 2018. http://www.facebook.com.

———. "Public commentary about Gina's Italian Kitchen." Accessed August 14, 2018. http://www.facebook.com.

———. "Public commentary about Hyde's." Accessed August 17, 2018. http://www.facebook.com.

———. "Public commentary about Isgro's Ristorante Italiano." Accessed August 14, 2018. http://www.facebook.com.

———. "Public commentary about the Manchester Inn." Accessed August 14, 2018. http://www.facebook.com.

———. "Public commentary about Milillo's Pizza." Accessed August 10, 2018. http://www.facebook.com.

———. "Public commentary about The Hickory Hut." Accessed August 13, 2018. http://www.facebook.com.

"Famous Middletown Hotel Closes." WCPO, January 4, 2011. Accessed August 18, 2018. http://www.wcpo.com.

Find a Grave. "Elmer Nichting Obituary." Accessed August 15, 2018. http://www.findagrave.com.

———. "Felix Isgro Obituary." Accessed August 15, 2018. http://www.findagrave.com.

———. "Yolanda Schiavone Obituary." Accessed August 15, 2018. http://www.findagrave.com.

Gambrell, Mandy. "Fire Is Third in Five Years at Hamilton Coffee Shop." *Journal-News,* January 10, 2013. Accessed August 28, 2018. http://www.journalnews.com.

Gillett, Rachel. "17 Weird Jobs You Probably Didn't Know Exist." *Business Insider*, March 14, 2017. Accessed August, 25, 2018. https://www.businessinsider.com/weird-jobs-you-probably-didnt-know-about-2017-3.

Gorn, Elliott J. *Dillinger's Wild Ride: The Year That Made America's Public Enemy Number One.* Oxford, UK: Oxford University Press, 2009.

Grant, Tom. "Jolly's Root Beer Opening Is One Sure Sign of Spring." *Journal-News.*

———. "Nichting's Dining Review." *Journal-News*, February 3, 1977. Accessed August 10, 2018. http://www.newspapers.com.

Harrison, Ed. "Out and About Dining Review with Ed Harrison/Isgro's Ristorante Italiano." *Journal-News*, September 20, 1974. Accessed August 12, 2018. http://www.newspapers.com.

Henderson, Dick. Interview with author conducted June 27, 2018.

Hyde's Restaurant. "Our History." Accessed August 19, 2018. http://www.hydespies.com.

Internet Movie Data Base. "Profile of Johnny Black." Accessed August 19, 2018. http://www.imdb.com/johnnyblack.

Isgro, Gina. Interview with author conducted June, 18, 2018.

Isgro, Vince. "History of Isgro's Ristorante Italiano." Accessed August 12, 2018. http://www.facebook.com.

Italian American Social Club. "Italian Immigration at Ellis Island (1892–1954)." Accessed August 7, 2018. http://www.iascorlando.org.

Johnson, Paula. "Hidden Flavors—Find the Meadows in Middletown." Accessed August 27, 2018. http://www.daytoncitypaper.com.

Jolivette, Greg. Interview with author conducted June 29, 2018.

Kramer, Karen Underwood. Interview with author conducted June 29, 2018.

Kramer, Ronda. Interview with author conducted April 24, 2018.

Kreger, Elizabeth. Interview with author conducted June, 24, 2018.

"Last Day for Texas Celebrated Drive-Ins." The History Channel, November 14, 2006. Accessed August 21, 2018. http://www.history.com.

Library of Congress. "The Great Arrival—Immigration—Italian." Accessed August 7, 2018. http://www.loc.gov.

Lindenwald Kiwanis. "Club History." Accessed August 19, 2018. http://www.lindenwaldkiwanis.org.

Lum's. "History of Lum's." Accessed August 28, 2018. http://www.google.com.

McCrabb, Rick. "Manchester Inn Waitress Loses Her Second Home." *Journal-News*, January 15, 2011. Accessed August 18, 2018. http://www.journalnews.com.

———. "Middletown Restaurant to Open with New Owners." *Journal-News*, May 27, 2014. Accessed August 20, 2018. http://www.journalnews.com.

———. "7 Restaurants That Are Missed in Butler County." *Journal-News*, December 29, 2017. Accessed August 28, 2018. http://www.journalnews.com.

McDermott, Natalie Schiavone. Interview with author conducted July 3, 2018.

McDulin, Bill. "Got a Minute?" *Journal-News*, December 3, 1975.

The Meadows. "About Us." Accessed August 20, 2018. http://www.meadows1934.com.

Mealey, Lorri. "The History of American Restaurants in the 20th Century." The Balance, June 21, 2018. Accessed August 16, 2018. http://www.thebalance.com.

———. "What Makes a Restaurant Family Style." The Balance, June 18, 2018. Accessed August 16, 2018. http://www.thebalance.com.

Metthe, Claire. "Butler County Ohio Misses the Hickory Hut." Butler County, Ohio, July 21, 2018. Accessed August 27, 2018. http://www.butlercountyohious.com.

Milders, Tully. Interview with author conducted April 24, 2018.

Milillo, Frank. Interview with author conducted June 19, 2018.

Nichting, Marlene. Interview with author conducted June 11, 2018.

Ohio History Central. "Butler County." Accessed August 7, 2018. http://www.ohiohistorycentral.org.

———. "Fairfield, Ohio." Accessed August 7, 2018. http://www.ohiohistorycentral.org.

———. "Hamilton, Ohio." Accessed August 7, 2018. http://www.ohiohistorycentral.org.

———. "Italian Ohioans." Accessed August 7, 2018. http://www.ohiohistorycentral.org.

———. "Middletown, Ohio." Accessed August 7, 2018. http://www.ohiohistorycentral.org.

———. "Oxford, Ohio." Accessed August 7, 2018. http://www.ohiohistorycentral.org.

Osborne, Donnie. Interview with author conducted June 27, 2018.

Pack, Lauren. "Sorg Mansion Restoration Taking Shape in Middletown." Journal-News, July 18, 2016. Accessed August 28, 2018. http://www.journalnews.com.

Pittman, Michael. "Former Butler County Judge Dies at 82." Journal-News, June 19, 2014. Accessed August 18, 2018. http://www.journalnews.com.

Rauber, Jennifer Bowermaster. Interview with author conducted July 10, 2018.

Robinette, Eric. "Bristol Palin Knocks Middletown." Journal-News, July 1, 2011. Accessed August 18, 2018. http://www.journalnews.com.

Sammicheledibari, Italy. Accessed August 7, 2018. http://www.comune.sammicheledibari.ba.it.

Schiavone, Frank III. Interview with author conducted July 3, 2018.

Schiavone, Frank IV. Interview with author conducted July 3, 2018.

Schneider, Chris Riemen. "21st Century Supper Clubs." Star Tribune, March 12, 2009. Accessed August 15, 2018. http://www.startribune.com.

Schwartzberg, Eric. "The Jug, Landmark Drive-in Eatery, Celebrates 80 Years." *Journal-News*, July 19, 2012. Accessed August 28, 2018. http://www.journalnews.com.

Smallwood, Mary Jo Lambros. Interview with author conducted June 29, 2018.

Smith, Andrew F. *The Oxford Companion to American Food and Drink*. Oxford, UK: Oxford University Press, 2007.

Snyder, Cindy Boyd. Interview with author conducted April 24, 2018.

Stout, Ronald. Interview with author conducted June 28, 2018.

TheaterOrgans.com. "The Moon River Organ." Accessed August 20, 2018. http://www.theaterorgans.com/ohio/WLW.com.

Thomas, Larry. "Dining Review on Isgro's Ristorante Italiano." *Journal-News*, October 11, 1973. Accessed August 14, 2018. http://www.newspapers.com.

Tweh, Bowdeya. "Middletown Hotel's New Owner Plans Historic Renovation." Cincinnati.com, September 27, 2014. Accessed August 18, 2018. http://www.cincinnati.com.

Underwood, Richard. Interview with author conducted June 29, 2018.

Vaughn, Daniel. "The History of the Pig Stands, America's Motor Lunch." *Texas Monthly*, February 18, 2015. Accessed August 21, 2018. http://www.texasmonthly.com.

Weaver, Skip. Interview with author conducted April 24, 2018.

Williams, Ken. "Shady Nook Just Is One of a Kind." *Journal-News*, September 12, 1976. Accessed August 20, 2018. http://www.newspapers.com.

Wren, Keith. Interview with author conducted July 9, 2018.

Wyatt, R.L. "Lunchtime at Deuscher's—Dixie Hamburgers, Belly Bombers or Dead Goats?" Growing up on Prytania (blog). November 1, 2015. https://growinguponprytania.wordpress.com/2015/11/01/lunchtime-at-deuschers-dixie-hamburgers-belly-bombers-or-dead-goats/.

INDEX

J

Jolly's 7, 108, 110, 112, 113, 114, 115
Jug, the 115

K

Kostas Restaurant 130

L

Lakeside Inn 130
Liberty Restaurant, the 131
Lum's 79, 131

M

Manchester Inn, the 64
Meadows, the 94
Mel's 131
Milders Inn, the 13
Milillo's 7, 22, 23, 24, 25, 26, 28, 30, 32, 33, 129
Millville Restaurant, the 131

N

Nichting's 58

P

Pusch's Family Restaurant 131

R

Rainbow Gardens, the 131
Red's Hamburgers 131
Richard's Pizza 81

S

Schiavone's 20, 47, 48, 49, 50, 51, 52
Shady Nook 70
Symmes Tavern 13

V

Venice Castle 132

W

Waldo's 64

ABOUT THE AUTHOR

Teri Horsley's combined love of history, food and writing led to the creation of this book. As a former restaurant critic and food reporter for the Cox Ohio Newspaper Group, Horsley spent much time with Butler County chefs to learn the secrets behind their great meals and help them take their message to the public. She also wrote hundreds of articles for local, regional and national magazines. Her first book, *The Milders Inn of Fairfield, Ohio: Gangsters, Baseball & Fried Chicken*, was published by The History Press in 2016. The book focused on the fascinating history of a Fairfield, Ohio restaurant and the notorious patrons who dined there.

After earning her master's degree in public history from Northern Kentucky University in 2015, Horsley discovered a passion for digital storytelling, and she expanded her writing career into producing documentary films, winning several national awards for her two short films, *Smacked* and *Extraordinary Vision*. In addition, she will earn a second master's degree in film producing from Regent University in 2020. In addition to her creative spirit, Horsley has an interest in advertising and marketing and works as the Ohio sales manager for Porter Advertising, which is based in Hamilton, Ohio, and Richmond, Indiana. In her work as an advertising specialist, Horsley helps numerous clients, including many restaurants, develop a marketing strategy to ensure their continued success in the region.

With her love of food, Horsley spends much of her free time honing her hobby of cooking, working with many regional chefs to expand her abilities. With her favorite cuisines being Mediterranean and Mexican,

Horsley spends much time in cooking classes as she learns how to perfect delicious meals.

In addition to her cooking interests, Horsley loves to travel and spends part of most vacations taking recreational cooking classes; as such, she has cooked all over the United States. Her other hobbies include gardening and playing competitive trivia, and she is currently working on obtaining her private pilot's license. Horsley grew up and continues to live in Hamilton, Ohio, and she remains very active on social media, promoting area chefs and cooking schools to enhance their visibility within the local community.